The Power Of Funding

The Power Of Funding

In the Hair and Beauty Business

Sarah Abel

authors
AND CO.

First published in Great Britain in 2024
by Authors & Co.
www.authorsandco.pub

ISBN 978-1-915771-92-6 (paperback)

Contents

Introduction — The Journey Begins

This book came about because I have been asked repeatedly: "How do you get funding for training?" I realised a lot of people find the whole idea overwhelming; this is a shame because there are so many small training providers and businesses out there doing amazing work but getting left behind.

At the core of it, I am a big believer in teaming up and sharing what we know to help each other grow. That is what this book is all about: breaking down the entire process of getting funded into bite-sized pieces. I want to clear up the confusion around all the red tape - stuff like audits, inspections and all those rules we need to follow.

I want to break down the financial side of starting a funded training business like mine, so you know what you are getting into. Back when I began, things were more straightforward. My first real funding came from apprenticeship schemes, which, to be honest, are still one of the best and most reliable ways to get started.

Regardless of which government is in charge, apprenticeships remain a cornerstone of training and can lead to many other funding opportunities. But fast forward to 2024, and the landscape for newcomers has changed dramatically. The bureaucracy and red tape involved in securing funding have grown significantly, making it all too easy for people to feel overwhelmed and consider giving up. That is exactly why I felt compelled to write this book. I wanted to offer a helping hand to guide you through deciding whether to pursue a direct contract or explore other, less bureaucratic ways to fund your training business.

But, hey, this is not meant to scare you off; it is the opposite. I want to show you the ropes so you'll think about teaming up with me. Together, we could do some great work, offering quality, fit-for-purpose training programmes that could make a real difference.

I'm talking about building something where we all win - you, me, and the people we're training. Even when times are tough, this kind of training can be a lifeline for people looking to skill up without breaking the bank. And I'll be straight with you—this book will also spell out how this can make good business sense, bringing in steady monthly income while keeping things above board.

So, what is this book going to give you? Well, it's like a treasure map for setting up a funded training academy that will attract attention and support.

I've used this roadmap to grow my own seven-figure training business, eventually stepping back from daily operations with a clear exit plan in place. When I am ready, this plan will allow me to sell the business for six to eight times the net profit, ensuring a comfortable retirement.

This seven-step roadmap includes:

- **Robust Foundations**: The critical building blocks for creating a solid and scalable funded training business structure.
- **Opportunities for Funding**: Where to find funding and how to effectively tender for it, giving your business the financial boost it needs.
- **Accreditation**: How to develop regulated and high-quality training programs that qualify for the largest funding opportunities.
- **Dream Team**: Using funding to grow skills and development within your business while getting paid to do so.
- **Marketing & Sales Strategy**: Techniques to attract funders and the financial resources to grow, while simultaneously drawing in clients to sustain them.
- **Attitude & Growth Mindset**: Business can be tough, and as you grow, you will need to develop various mindsets to navigate challenges. This chapter dives into these mental shifts and how to manage them, even in tough times.
- **Programs, Policies & Procedures**: An overview of the essential elements funders expect from you, ensuring you're ready to work with them.

But this isn't about the money. It's a journey, from starting in the training game to building something that can stand. I've been down this road, from buying my first little salon to steering through the chaos of the financial crash and beyond. It's been quite a ride, and I've picked up useful stuff along the way.

This isn't just a guide to making quick cash. It's about setting up something you can be proud of; something that can keep ticking over and even allow you to step back when you're ready. Whether you're dreaming of hitting that six-figure income or have even bigger plans, the key is to know what you're aiming for—your own personal "money pot" that keeps you driven.

And for anyone who has ever considered investing in funded training but got cold feet because it all seemed too complex, this book is for you. I want to take the mystery out of the entire process, showing you a clear path to setting up a funded training academy that fits right into what you are already doing.

By the end of this book, I hope you will see the potential in funded training, not just as a business opportunity but to make a difference. And the best part? You do not have to go it alone. I am here to help guide you through, making the entire process smoother and more rewarding. My goal is to find people who would love to work with us long-term and who cannot be bothered with all the bureaucratic stuff, so we will help you to take the pain out of funded training.

Ready to dive in? Let's leave behind any doubts or worries you have and take the first step of this journey together.

Chapter 1

Robust Foundations: Why you Need Them

The journey to building a thriving revenue in the business sector often gets attributed to proficiency in sales and marketing alone. In my experience, focusing on these areas nearly doubled my income, highlighting their significance. However, the foundation of a lasting training business that attracts funding goes much deeper. In this chapter, we'll explore the critical elements of creating solid training revenue by leveraging government funding, supported by strategic planning, vision and core values—all through my personal experiences and insights.

My adventure into funded training began out of sheer frustration. As a small salon owner, expanding my team has always been a significant challenge. The candidates

I encountered typically fell into two categories: those with the necessary skills but who didn't align with my business ethos, and those with the right attitude but who lacked the required skills.

Initially, I focused on hiring a team with the requisite skills. However, I soon realised that these individuals were often resistant to learning new procedures and lacked the passion for growth that I valued. My goal was to develop a team that would not only contribute to a profitable revenue stream but also enhance their skills in customer service, marketing, and sales. This would, in turn, foster a sustainable and profitable client base.

In response to this challenge, I shifted my strategy to hiring unskilled but culturally compatible individuals. This approach, however, meant investing heavily in their training. Unfortunately, after receiving the training, many of these employees left to become independent contractors elsewhere, leaving me feeling that my investment was unappreciated and unrewarded.

It was during this time that I discovered apprenticeship programs. However, there were no apprenticeship opportunities available for nail technicians, so I set a goal to create one. I quickly realized that to access government funding, I needed to obtain minimum qualifications, including the "Preparing to Teach in the Lifelong Learning Sector" qualification, now known as the "Award in Education," as well as qualifications in assessment. In the early 2000s, I had to fund these qualifications myself. Thankfully, today there is funding available for these qualifications—if you know where to look, which I do. Yes, it can be funded through apprenticeship funding or even advanced loans.

After qualifying as a teacher and assessor, I was awarded a modest fund by a local training provider. However, to utilise the amount awarded, I needed to find other salons interested in taking on nail apprentices. Drawing on the sales figures from the apprentices I had already trained, I visited salons in my local area and showcased the benefits of adding a funding stream through nail services. I highlighted the advantages, including a £1,000 government grant available to businesses—even if they wanted to upskill an existing team member. This approach enabled me to train not only my own staff but also staff from other local salons in nail services. This marked the beginning of the strategy that I still use today.

I think of it as educating my competition while collaborating with other businesses to grow their teams through government funding. Whether you're just starting or are an established business owner looking to scale, my goal is to help you build a business model with a clear exit plan. By utilising the various government funding options available, you can make your business so attractive that when the time comes to sell, you'll command top prices. For example, I recently had my business valued at six times its net profit, and I'm still working on it. This valuation would give me £1,500,000 based on our current net profit after excluding my salary—and I do not even work in the business anymore. I employ 17 people, and the business continues to thrive under their management.

But first, we need to lay the foundations so your business can grow, scale, and thrive. Let's get started!

Laying the Groundwork: Strategy and Vision

A journey of a thousand miles begins with a single step, and in business, that first step is the creation of a clear, strategic vision. My venture into the business world was no different. I quickly realised that sales and marketing alone couldn't guarantee long-term success; the initial excitement of rising sales figures soon gave way to the sobering reality that without a solid foundation, the business was like a house of cards, vulnerable to the slightest adversity.

When dealing with government funding, a solid foundation is crucial. Funders will assess not only the sustainability of the partners they support but also the culture and financial health of your business—factors that can make or break your bid. That's why it's essential to start with a clear vision of what you want to achieve. This vision becomes your story, guiding and shaping your bids. Remember: the people reviewing your bids are human, too. It's your responsibility to ensure they understand and connect with your goals, as well as see how they align with theirs.

By sharing your vision effectively, you can build a compelling narrative that resonates with decision-makers. Let's explore how you can craft that vision and lay the groundwork for a business that not only thrives but withstands the test of time.

The Importance of Strategy and Vision

Discovering the necessity of a clear strategy and vision for my business was a pivotal moment for me. My business had become stagnant and stopped growing. To be entirely transparent, the reason for this stagnation was the lack of a coherent plan to secure the funding needed for growth. Our actions were often reactive—chasing available funding or setting arbitrary goals, like enrolling twenty new students in a month—without any long-term vision. This approach left us without a clear direction, and as a result, we failed to grow.

When COVID-19 hit in 2020, it served as a wake-up call, revealing the precarious position my business was in because there was no clear strategic plan. My goal was for the business to reach a scale where I could either sell it or have it run independently by a team, allowing me to step back and only attend quarterly board meetings. However, at fifty-six years old, I recognised a critical flaw: the business was overly reliant on me. I was the heart of operations, from securing contracts to driving growth, making the business unattractive to potential buyers without me in the picture.

This realisation was daunting, and my confidence was further shaken by the gap between theory and practice in business management—a disparity I encountered through conversations on platforms like Clubhouse. It became clear that while many could talk a good game, few could deliver results.

During this period of introspection, I met Danny Wicks, a specialist in team development. Despite having a team of fifteen, it became evident that they were not aligned with my vision or values, often leading to frustration on my part. Their dependence on me for decisions highlighted a lack of ownership and clarity about the business's direction, which I realised reflected my own uncertainty.

Engaging with Danny and his business partner at the time, Graham Hardy, was a turning point. They introduced us to essential systems and processes that helped clarify our vision and funding strategy. With his guidance, we defined where we saw the business in the next four to five years, with my initial goal being to retire. This vision has since evolved, but the strategic framework we established has remained a cornerstone of our decision-making process.

This strategic overhaul transformed our business. Our funding pots doubled, and every decision made since then has been aligned with our long-term vision, from investments in training to hiring decisions. This focus on the future underscores the importance of a clear vision and a robust strategy to achieve it.

A key lesson from this journey is the significance of breaking down financial goals into tangible targets, such as student numbers or funding revenue sources, to make the vision achievable. Moreover, it is crucial to ensure that any investment, whether in funding or resources, aligns with the end goal, avoiding distractions that do not contribute to the overarching vision.

During the aftermath of COVID-19, under Danny's mentorship, we embarked on a mission to realign our business with a clear vision and strategy. This entailed a comprehensive session with our team to lay out our objectives, including the expansion of our team and the specific qualities we sought in new hires to bolster our management structure. We delved into our sales goals, pinpointing where these sales and funding sources originated from and scrutinising our offerings to identify profitable ventures versus those that were not contributing to our bottom line.

Our strategy was meticulously planned, identifying the resources, properties, and the type of government funding needed to achieve our targets. This marked a pivotal shift in our approach to working with partners, enabling us to expand our sales by offering funding opportunities where we shared the benefits through commissions and bonuses. This new direction required a thorough understanding of our operational needs—from space requirements to logistical considerations—ensuring that everything aligned with our overarching vision.

To maintain focus and drive continuous progress, we adopted a twelve-week planning cycle. This approach allowed us to set specific short-term objectives within the broader context of our annual goals, ensuring that each quarter brought us closer to our ultimate vision. This method was particularly effective for me, as it curbed my tendency to chase new opportunities that did not align with our strategic objectives—a habit that had previously hindered our growth.

For example, we once pursued a tender in another county, offered by a different training provider. However, we lacked the team and resources needed to deliver the training to a high standard, resulting in a loss rather than a profit. By implementing a clear strategy and focusing on funding opportunities that aligned with our core offerings, we were able to avoid such pitfalls and concentrate on opportunities that provided the greatest returns. This disciplined approach ensured that we targeted funding that truly matched our strengths and objectives.

This structured approach goes beyond business operations; it embodies our core mission to empower small businesses to develop their teams internally and generate additional revenue through training. This mission has been the foundation of our business since its inception and continues to guide our decisions and strategies. We have developed programs for our companies, enabling them to access free funding for their training needs rather than relying on their resources. This approach allows business owners to eventually replace themselves while driving sales through strategic funding opportunities.

Our website echoes this mission, stating our commitment to “empowering creative minds” This encompasses our desire to help individuals achieve a balance between their professional aspirations and personal lives, enabling them to spend more time with their families and pursue their passions. Our success stories, reflected in the testimonials of those who have grown from apprentices in salons to salon owners themselves, are a testament to the impact of our vision and mission.

One standout example is a salon in Sittingbourne, 'Boniface', where the owner, a former student of ours, has utilised our training programmes to develop her team and expand her business. This journey from assessor apprentice to salon owner and now to expanding further into new salons exemplifies the realisation of our vision.

The transition from an ad-hoc approach to a strategic, vision-driven one was transformative. It not only doubled our sales in two years but also instilled a forward-looking mindset throughout every aspect of the business. This shift underscores the power of a clear vision and a detailed strategy in guiding business decisions and achieving long-term success.

In summary, our mission and strategy have not only shaped the direction of our business but profoundly influenced the lives of those we have worked with. By staying true to our vision and meticulously planning our steps, we have managed to create a thriving ecosystem that supports growth, innovation and personal fulfilment.

Core Values Drive your Business

The next big step was identifying our core values and embedding them deeply within the culture of our training business. This has been a transformative experience, especially since returning from the COVID-19 closures. I remember a piece of advice I received years ago that I didn't fully grasp at the time: the values of your business not only shape the team you build but attract those who stay with you over the long haul. It is about creating a community of like-minded individuals, extending beyond just our team to include our clients as well. This alignment has proven crucial, as anyone not embodying our values often finds themselves out of sync with our culture, consuming my time and energy or eventually parting ways with us.

Our core values – Passion for Learning, Going Above and Beyond, Keeping it Real and Commitment to Success – were crafted through a collaborative effort between my co-director Julie and me. What was striking was when we asked our team about *their* values, their responses mirrored ours, not always in wording but certainly in spirit. This exercise highlighted the synergy within our team, reaffirming that we had indeed attracted individuals who shared our ethos.

These values have become the bedrock of our operations. They are not just words we revisit during team meetings; they are lived experiences that we encourage and celebrate. Whether it is 'Keeping it Real' with a challenging student or going 'Above and Beyond' to achieve excellence, these values are reflected in our day-to-day actions and decision-making processes.

This value-driven approach has extended beyond internal team dynamics to influence all aspects of our business, from client relationships to partnerships with stakeholders. When writing bids and engaging with outside stakeholders, such as funders and accreditation bodies like Ofsted, our commitment to these values has not gone unnoticed. We have been congratulated on our approach, and 'Keeping it Real' was even mentioned in a recent Ofsted report. I believe that these values and the fact that our team and clients understand them helped us secure our Grade 2 rating.

For instance, in our collaborations with other training providers or funders, we only engage with those who resonate with our values. This alignment has been crucial in maintaining the integrity and quality of our services. There have been times when we needed to reassess relationships, making tough decisions to discontinue partnerships that did not align with our core values, but ensuring that our business remains true to its founding principles.

For example, we once worked with a funder who was consistently slow in responding to our queries and delayed in making payments. They provided inadequate guidance on how to use the paperwork they supplied and offered no additional training, even though we were willing to pay for it. This left us feeling frustrated and let down. I vividly remember waking up at 3 a.m. one morning, worrying about how I would pay my team after delivering three months of training without receiving payment. Thankfully, after much persistence and with the help of a kind mother-in-law who lent me the money, we were eventually paid. This experience reinforced the importance of working with partners who truly align with our values and priorities.

Our training business has foundations that are deeply rooted in our core values, which guide our interactions with students, employees and partners alike. Let's delve into how these values have practically shaped our business operations and culture.

Keeping It Real: This value is about transparency and honesty in all our communications, whether with students, clients or team members. For instance, when advising students or salon owners about what it truly takes to succeed, we lay out the realities—both the challenges and the rewards. This honesty fosters trust and informed decision-making, crucial for long-term retention, especially given that our funding is contingent on student completion rates. By maintaining this candidness, we not only build stronger relationships but align expectations with reality, enhancing satisfaction and success rates.

Commitment to Success: Commitment to excellence is a cornerstone of our ethos. While we have faced moments when our service did not meet this high bar, those instances became valuable learning opportunities. We strive to offer quality training, evident in the glowing testimonials and Google reviews from our clients. These affirmations not only validate our efforts but motivate our team to continually elevate the quality of our training and services.

Going Above and Beyond: Our sales team exemplifies this value through their dedication to meeting ambitious targets, such as fulfilling the adult education budget within set timelines to ensure growth for the following year. Their willingness to go the extra mile, working tirelessly to exceed these goals, reflects a collective commitment to the business's success. This ethos of perseverance is mirrored in our strategic pivots and innovations, especially when faced with funding changes or other challenges, underscoring a resolve to not only survive but thrive.

Passion for Learning: This value permeates our entire operation, from the continuous development of our team members to the delivery of our courses. We invest in the growth of every individual, whether they are stepping into the world of hairdressing or advancing into leadership roles. Utilising the apprenticeship scheme, we provide structured, quality training that culminates in valuable qualifications for our team. This commitment to development ensures consistent quality across our services and fosters a culture of lifelong learning.

Incorporating these values into our daily operations has not only strengthened our training business internally but enhanced our reputation and relationships externally. By living these values, we have cultivated a robust, value-driven culture that propels us towards our future goals, ensuring our training business's longevity and success.

In summary, infusing our core values into every facet of our business has shaped our team and client base and guided our partnerships and operational decisions. This alignment has steered our business towards sustainable growth, ensuring that we remain focused on what truly matters: creating a cohesive, value-driven community that thrives on mutual respect, continuous learning and a relentless pursuit of excellence.

Chapter 2

Due Diligence: Your Safety Net

To scale a business using funding, it's essential to collaborate with other training providers who also hold direct contracts with the government. Access to these larger funding pools is crucial for expanding your business. For example, in 2023, our funding pot awarded by the Education and Skills Funding Agency for adult learners was just under £500k, which we fully utilised within seven months. Our strategy is to consistently seek out additional adult funding from other training providers who are underspending their allocations. If these providers do not use their funds, they must return them to the Treasury at the end of the year, often resulting in a smaller allocation the following year. By writing a solid tender, you can position yourself as a valuable partner, making them eager to work with you to ensure they spend their allocated funds effectively.

These opportunities often arise throughout the year, so we have found it beneficial to invest in a company that specialises in writing bids and identifying available funding on a monthly basis. By tendering for additional contracts with other training providers who also hold direct contracts, we access more funding and significantly grow our business. Also, working with different training providers helped us build a proven record of accomplishment of delivery, achievements, and successful outcomes—such as students completing our programs. This proven success increases your chances of winning both direct contracts and subcontracts, which is vital for growth and opens additional funding opportunities to continue scaling your business.

Picking the right people to partner with was quite a learning curve. My first experience with a specific college underscored the importance of thorough due diligence. Despite taking a hefty cut of the profits, they provided little in return and failed to compensate me for £10,000 worth of work. That was a harsh lesson in the consequences of not vetting partners properly.

Another way to grow your provision is by partnering with satellite centres. Traditionally, expanding our provision would require purchasing additional premises and recruiting a significant number of staff. However, by collaborating with other training providers or trainers who do not hold government contracts but are eager to access them, we can achieve growth more efficiently. From past experiences, I've learned valuable lessons that have shaped our approach, so it's important to be cautious and strategic in these partnerships.

One key lesson we learned was the necessity of investing time upfront in training our trainers and their teams, including those at our satellite centres. After some trial and error, we developed a paid program that not only teaches other training providers how to access funding for themselves but also allows us to cherry-pick potential subcontractors. By teaching them upfront what they need in place, we ensure they are well-prepared. We pay them to deliver training under our umbrella, much like a franchise, until they have the capability to handle larger contracts and become subcontractors in their own right.

This approach is a win-win for both parties. We get to train them in our systems and processes, as well as the essentials of funding compliance, all with our ongoing support. Since they pay an upfront fee, we know they are invested and committed to putting in the necessary time. At the end of the program, they complete an accredited qualification, meeting all our due diligence requirements. This not only qualifies them to bid for contracts with us but also with other training providers, confident that they have the systems, processes, and capabilities that are required in a subcontractor.

I've come to value collaboration deeply, treating all satellite partners as integral members of our team. This mindset extends beyond simply delivering funded courses; it involves sharing our systems and processes to foster mutual growth. When seeking a partner, prioritise their reputation, willingness to improve systems and collaborative spirit.

Make sure to thoroughly review their records at Companies House, check their Ofsted grade, and read reviews online and through word of mouth. Ask to see their filed accounts for the last three years and do a business credit check.

The following checklist will help determine if they have what you are looking for as a subcontractor: if they have not, send them to us for training.

A) Which awarding body or bodies do you use to register the learners you teach under your current contract?

B) Are you responsible for your own registrations with the awarding body?

C) Is your centre with the awarding bodies in your company name or that of your lead provider?

D) Do you have Direct Claims with your awarding bodies, and what is your current risk rating?

E) Who is responsible for the quality assurance of the qualifications - yourself or the lead provider?

F) How often does the lead provider visit you to conduct monitoring and lesson observations?

G) How often do you hold meetings with the lead provider to report on progress and any issues?

H) What is the minimum standard expected for the retention of learners and timely completion under your contract?

I) What is the minimum standard expected for the retention of learners and timely completion under your contract?

J) What due diligence process does your lead provider follow?

K) Do you have a UKPRN?

L) What type of provider are you registered as on the APAR – Main, Supporting or Employer?

M) What level of public liability, professional indemnity, and employer liability insurance do you hold?

N) Are you Matrix accredited?

O) Are you Cyber Security registered and compliant?

P) Do you have a current sustainability policy and action plan?

Q) Are you registered with a carbon footprint tracking organisation or working towards net zero?

R) Do you have an ICO registration certificate?

S) Are you currently an ESFA, Job Centre Plus or DWP Accredited provider?

T) Have you ever been subject to or included as a subcontractor in an Ofsted visit, and if so, what grading was achieved?

U) Do you produce an annual Self-Assessment Report and Quality Improvement Plan and how often do you review/update it?

V) What values of contracts do you currently deliver?

W) Can you provide references from funded training providers you have delivered training for

X) Can you produce financial reports and cashflow and profit lost forecasts?

These are just a few starting questions I would be asking before I even thought about working with someone, but

I would recommend compiling a due diligence file using policies and procedures that I will teach in this book, asking them to evidence this.

If you're not quite ready for direct funding yet aligning with a reputable provider simplifies the learning process and accelerates progress. And don't forget to seek guidance from mentors who have walked a similar path; their insights can significantly ease your journey.

Chapter 3
Financial Health and Planning

Importance of a Clear Financial Plan

Before you try and skip this chapter, be warned: it's **Very, Very** important that you read it. The next part is vital because, without it, you won't secure a contract, no matter how good your training is—funders will want to know that you understand your numbers.

This was a challenge for me. I hated dealing with numbers, but I knew how crucial they were. So, I made it a priority to educate myself and ensure I knew them inside out.

People find this part boring to learn, and I'm sure you might feel the same.

However, I've realised that understanding the numbers also gives me peace of mind. My finance director creates easy-to-read graphs that simplify the data, and we even share these with the training businesses we work with, teaching them this critical aspect thoroughly.

Having a clear financial plan is crucial for any business, but especially when tendering for large contracts or applying to become an apprenticeship or training provider. A financial plan not only helps you understand your current financial position, forecast future performance and make informed business decisions, but demonstrates the financial health of your business to the funder.

Key components of a financial plan include:

Profit and Loss (P&L) Statement: This document summarises your revenues, costs and expenses over a specific period, typically a month, quarter or year. It helps you determine whether your business is profitable and where adjustments may be needed.

Twelve-Month Cash Flow Forecast: This forecast projects your business's cash inflow and outflow over the next year. It helps you anticipate periods of cash shortages or surpluses, ensuring you can manage your finances effectively and avoid liquidity issues.

If I'm honest, years ago, I wouldn't have been able to tell you much about my numbers. I relied too heavily on my accountant, which was a big mistake. It led to owing the taxman £56,000 because I was spending too much of the money I was making, instead of setting it aside. I wasn't keeping a close eye on our profits and cash flow.

I often ask founders about their cash flow and profit and loss, and they rarely know these figures week to week. This is a big mistake that can cost you not only money but also the chance to secure funding contracts. It's crucial to get into the habit of staying on top of your finances.

During COVID, I read the book *Profit First*, which was a game-changer. My good friend Jo Simpson, who runs the Financial Growth Academy UK on Instagram, now teaches these principles to small businesses. If you haven't checked her out, I highly recommend it. Thanks to these insights, I now get pretty excited that our profit and taxes are all accounted for. It helps me sleep at night!

So, depending on your goals, what should you be measuring closely and working regularly to reduce or grow? My business mentor Danny always said, "Scale, but keep your business lean." Remember to invest in your growth but stay on track with your numbers. It is all about finding that balance: growing sales while keeping an eye on costs. This approach has been crucial in my journey and it's something I can't stress enough. Keep things lean, invest wisely and always stay on top of your financials.

Here is how I break it down:

Financial Overview

Revenue: List all sources of income from your business activities, such as sales, training fees and grants.

Cost of Goods Sold (COGS): Include direct costs related to providing your services or products, such as materials and instructor fees.

Gross Profit: Subtract COGS from Revenue (this is your gross profit - try to keep this as high as possible).

Operating Expenses: Itemise expenses like rent, utilities, marketing and administrative costs.

Net Profit: Subtract Operating Expenses from Gross Profit.

Example Template:

Description	Amount
Revenue	£100,00
COGS	-£40,000
Gross Profit	£60,000
Operating Expenses	-£30,000
Net Profit	£30,000

12-Month Cash Flow Forecast

Starting Cash Balance: Begin with the cash you have on hand.

Cash Inflows: Forecast monthly revenue, loan receipts and any other cash sources.

Cash Outflows: Forecast monthly expenses, including both fixed and variable costs.

Net Cash Flow: Subtract total outflows from total inflows for each month.

Ending Cash Balance: Add Net Cash Flow to the Starting Cash Balance to get the Ending Cash Balance for each month.

Example Template:

Month	Starting Balance	Cash Inflows	Cash Outflows	Net Cash Flow	Ending Balance
Jan	£10,000	£15,000	-£12,000	£3,000	£13,000
Feb	£13,000	£15,000	-£14,000	£1,000	£14,000
...	...	...	...	...	...

Value of Financial Documents

- **Informed Decision-Making:** Financial documents provide a clear picture of your business's financial health, enabling you to make strategic decisions.
- **Budgeting and Planning:** They help in setting realistic budgets and planning for future growth.
- **Risk Management:** Anticipating cash flow issues helps in taking proactive measures to mitigate financial risks.
- **Investor Confidence:** Detailed financial plans instil confidence in potential investors or stakeholders about the viability of your business.

Course Profitability Analysis

Measuring the Profitability of Individual Courses:

The Value of Financial Documents

Informed Decision-Making: Financial documents provide a clear picture of your business's financial health, enabling you to make strategic decisions. For example, this month we know that because a lot of our council funding is often paid three to five months after we deliver the training, we need to replace the sales that month with instant cash. We therefore offer our private clients additional bonuses if they pay in full, which gives us the cash injection we need to cover the delay in payments.

Budgeting and Planning: These documents help us set realistic budgets and enable us to plan for future investments in tools and additional training for our team. By managing risk, we can anticipate cash flow issues and proactively mitigate financial risks.

Risk Management: Detailed financial plans allow us to stay ahead of potential cash flow problems. For instance, knowing that certain payments will be delayed helps us plan accordingly and find alternative funding sources, as I mentioned above.

Investor Confidence: Having detailed financial plans instils confidence in potential investors, stakeholders or funders about the viability of our business. This increases the chances of winning bids, contracts and funding, including loans.

Measuring the Profitability of Individual Courses

We break down the profitability of our courses by measuring several key factors:

- **Revenue per Course:** Track the total income generated from each course.
- **Direct Costs:** Calculate the direct expenses associated with delivering each course, such as tutor fees, materials and venue costs.
- **Indirect Costs:** Allocate a portion of overhead costs to each course based on usage or another relevant metric.
- **Net Profit per Course:** Subtract the total costs (direct and indirect) from the revenue to determine the profitability of each course.

Metrics and Methods:

- **Contribution Margin:** This is the difference between the revenue and the direct costs of a course. A higher contribution margin indicates a more profitable course.
- **Break-Even Analysis:** Determine the number of participants needed to cover the costs of running a course.
- **ROI (Return on Investment):** Measure the profitability relative to the cost of the course. Calculate as (Net Profit / Cost of Course) * 100%.

Influencing Decision-Making:

This approach allows us to prioritise courses with higher profitability and consider phasing out or redesigning less profitable ones. For example, we realised that running our customer service courses online and pre-recording the resources so clients can watch in their own time reduced tutor costs and minimised the need for written resources. This change made this course far more profitable and allowed us to enrol larger numbers.

It also helps us direct our resources, such as marketing efforts and tutor availability, towards courses that offer the highest returns. By using profitability analysis, we have been able to identify areas for improvement, like cost reduction or price adjustments, and plan for the expansion of popular and profitable courses. Moving these courses online instead of delivering them face-to-face has been a critical strategy.

Keeping track of these numbers and regularly reviewing them has enormously impacted our business's growth. It has allowed us to invest in scaling even larger and reward our current team, keeping them motivated and invested. This, in turn, improves the quality of the courses, as our tutors gain more experience. Consequently, we've seen improved outcomes and retention rates, which are crucial when operating with funding. Demonstrating retention and outcomes, such as achievements and progression, strengthens our ability to bid for contracts, as we clearly show we can deliver.

Financial Health and ESFA Requirements for Accessing Government Funding

Overview

It is crucial to stay on top of your business's financial health, especially when you want to use other people's money to fund your ventures and access government funding. This includes seeking support from organisations like the Education and Skills Funding Agency (ESFA) and the Department for Education (DfE). This lesson hit home for me early on after accumulating £75,000 in credit card debt. Even though I secured a contract, I was always upfront about my financial background. In fact, in 2015, a local council awarded us an interest-free growth loan. Despite initially facing scepticism from a panel of older men who didn't understand the hair and beauty sector, I managed to secure a £40,000 loan to grow my academy in Folkestone. Honesty and transparency were key.

If you're reading this and doubting that anyone would give you money, stop right there. Your past doesn't define your future. By learning from my experiences, you'll see that maintaining robust financial health is critical. This involves submitting comprehensive financial statements and adhering to strict guidelines set by funding bodies. Here is a summary of what you need to know and do to meet their requirements effectively:

Submission of Financial Statements

Annual Requirement: Submit your financial statements annually once they are finalised and signed.

Timelines: Delays in submission can result in an automatic 'Inadequate' financial health grade. Failure to submit within nine months of the period end, or upon ESFA/DfE request, can also lead to this grade.

Complete Financial Statements: Submissions must be full, audited (if required) and not abbreviated. They should include:

- Profit and Loss Account
- Balance Sheet
- Detailed notes to the accounts
- Breakdown of creditors and other creditors

Specific Guidelines for Businesses

Companies: Send full statutory accounts even if only abbreviated accounts are needed for Companies House. Why is this important to the ESFA? These accounts offer a transparent view of your company's financial health, showing compliance with legal requirements and building credibility. The ESFA relies on this information to assess financial stability, conduct risk assessments, and verify eligibility. Accurate statutory accounts are crucial for informed decision-making, influencing both the approval and terms of the funding your company may receive.

New Businesses:

- **Management Accounts**: If you lack statutory financial statements due to a lack of trading history, submit management accounts covering at least three months of actual trading activity and forecast figures for the remaining period, ensuring the total period covered is no less than one year.
- **Transition to Full Statements**: Submit full financial statements as soon as they are available. The initial financial health grade based on your management accounts is temporary and will be updated once your full statements are reviewed.

Grading and Compliance

External Sources: ESFA may use information from Companies House, credit reference agencies and monitoring sites to assess financial health.

Incomplete Submissions: Missing information can result in an 'Inadequate' grade due to insufficient data for a proper assessment.

Ongoing Assessment: Financial health grades based on management accounts will be reassessed once full financial statements are submitted.

Key Takeaways for New Businesses

- **Be Proactive**: Ensure financial statements are prepared, finalised and submitted promptly.
- **Ensure Completeness**: Submit full, detailed financial statements as required, not just extracts or summaries.
- **Prepare for Scrutiny**: Understand that incomplete or late submissions can severely impact your financial health grade and your eligibility for funding.
- **Maintain Accuracy**: Accurate and detailed financial records support better assessments and improve your chances of receiving and maintaining funding.

Financial Health

The ESFA uses financial health as a key measure of a business's financial status, assessing its performance and ability to meet ongoing financial commitments. This measure helps the ESFA understand the degree of risk involved in contracting with organisations, directly or indirectly. The financial health grade is crucial in determining the maximum recommended value of contracts suitable for a business's financial resources if they have a direct contract.

Financial health is graded based on financial ratios from the latest available and, where applicable, published financial statements. Every organisation must submit this information to the ESFA in accordance with its contract and application to a register, procurement or invitation to tender. For organisations with a contract with the ESFA/DfE, the latest financial statements must be sent to the ESFA promptly within strict annual deadlines.

Financial Health Elements

Financial health is graded based on three financial elements:

- **Profitability (sustainability)**: Assessed based on profit after tax as a percentage of turnover. Depreciation and amortisation are added back to profit after tax, and dividends are subtracted.
- **Solvency (current ratio)**: Assessed using the current ratio, which is the ratio between current assets and current liabilities.
- **Gearing (debt ratio)**: Based on debt as a percentage of reserves and debt.

Each of these elements is scored out of one hundred, by other training providers and funders and the education funding agency, and the combined score determines the overall financial health grade:

- **Outstanding**: 240 to 300 points
- **Good**: 180 to 230 points
- **Satisfactory**: 120 to 170 points
- **Inadequate**: <= 110 points

Recommended Funding Limit (RFL)

A key aspect of the financial health assessment is setting a maximum Recommended Funding Limit (RFL), which measures an organisation's financial capacity to deliver. The funding limit varies depending on whether the organisation is new or has an existing contract with the Education Skills Funding Agency and Department for Education. Other factors, such as infrastructure, may also impact a business's capacity to deliver.

To improve these scores, it's important to work on them. I have broken down how we continually do this, which then gives us access to bigger pots but also improves the profitability of our business—and let's be honest, the whole point of building a business is to eventually sell and retire and to live on the profits of the sale, is it not?

Improving Profitability (Sustainability):

Enhancing profitability is fundamental to the sustainability of any training business. To achieve this, focus on increasing revenue through strategic marketing, expanding product lines, or entering new markets. I will delve deeper into this when we discuss funding opportunities and marketing and sales strategies, including specific actions we've taken to create additional income streams. By doing this, you'll not only create a buffer against market fluctuations but also contribute to a more robust bottom line.

Equally important is cost management. Once a quarter, the finance director and I review our outgoings, identifying subscriptions and services we no longer need. For example, we've been using a specialist for our Facebook ads, but we discovered that this expert offers a course that someone on our marketing team could take. Although there's an initial investment, bringing this expertise in-house will reduce our outgoings over time. Additionally, we often find subscriptions we've forgotten to cancel. By bringing the team together to assess what is being used and what isn't, we can further reduce these costs.

Adjusting pricing strategies to reflect the true value provided, while staying competitive in the market, can further improve margins. Streamlining operations and investing in staff training to boost productivity will lead to greater efficiency and higher profitability. And here's the best part: apprenticeship schemes can help achieve this, and if you're the one providing the training, you'll get paid to do it. Based on my experience, this dual benefit is a powerful way to enhance both profitability and long-term sustainability.

Enhancing Solvency (Current Ratio):

Solvency, often measured by the current ratio, reflects a business's ability to meet its short-term obligations. Improving solvency starts with effective management of working capital, which includes speeding up receivables, extending payables without harming supplier relationships, and optimising inventory levels. One strategy we've implemented to increase current assets is introducing a paid program for some of our courses targeted at students who cannot access funding. By offering them additional value if they pay the full cost upfront, we've generated more cash payments, which has strengthened our current ratio and improved this aspect of the business.

On the liabilities side, reducing short-term debt and renegotiating payment terms with creditors can ease immediate financial pressures. Our finance director and quality manager review this monthly, examining various products we use to deliver training and negotiating with suppliers to extend payment terms where possible. Additionally, the senior management team reviews our financial position quarterly, exploring ways to reduce debt. For instance, we were recently approached by our bank, which offered us better interest rates and more favourable payment terms than another provider. By restructuring debt to extend the maturity of liabilities, we've been able to enhance our solvency, providing the business with more breathing room to operate effectively.

By continually improving our assets and managing liabilities, we ensure our financial position remains strong. This not only allows us to meet our obligations and keep growing, but it also keeps us attractive to funders. It's all about staying sharp, growing smart, and making sure we're always able to invest back into the business.

Improving Gearing (Debt Ratio)

Gearing, or the debt ratio, is a crucial measure of a company's financial leverage and risk. One straightforward way to improve gearing is by reducing debt, which can be accomplished by allocating more profits toward debt repayment or refinancing existing debt at lower interest rates. As I mentioned earlier, another effective approach is increasing equity—whether by retaining more earnings in the business or issuing new shares, businesses can strengthen their reserves and improve their financial position.

Controlling borrowing is equally important; taking on additional debt should be avoided unless it's necessary for growth and backed by solid cash flow projections. Exploring alternative financing options, such as equity financing or grants, can also help maintain a healthy balance between debt and equity, reducing financial risk and enhancing overall stability. You do this through equity financing: this can involve raising capital by selling shares in the company, which I did in the preliminary stages of my business to reduce debt and generate cash flow. By selling a few shares to my financial director and my husband's mum, I was able to bolster the company's reserves without the obligation of repaying debt or paying interest. This approach allowed me to reinvest in essential processes and systems that were crucial for our growth. Although it meant giving up a small part of ownership, the decision proved to be highly beneficial as it provided the financial stability needed to scale the business. Now, with the business having grown significantly, that early choice of equity financing has had a lasting positive impact, contributing to our success and expansion.

Chapter 4

Navigating the Maze of Funding Opportunities

In this chapter, I want to share more than just knowledge; I aim to tell a story of persistence, learning and mastery in securing funding for businesses. My journey is a testament to resilience and the art of navigating various funding opportunities, learning each bit, and harnessing them for sustained growth.

My journey into educational funding began with what seemed like a straightforward yet daunting task: registering as a training provider on the government's official website. This technical step was the gateway to numerous funding opportunities for those prepared to navigate the complexities of government and council grants. Initially, I was overwhelmed by the multitude of options, each with its own criteria and application processes. However, by breaking the task into manageable chunks, exploring the different funding streams became less intimidating.

To tackle these tasks, I employed the C.I.G.A.R. method, which stands for Current situation, Ideal situation, Gaps, Actions, and Review. This approach allowed me to systematically assess and address each challenge. Additionally, I used time blocking, a productivity technique where you allocate specific blocks of time to different tasks or activities throughout your day. Instead of working from a long to-do list, you schedule each task into a designated time-slot on your calendar. This method helps you focus on one thing at a time, reduces distractions, and ensures that important tasks receive the attention they need. By planning your day with time blocks, you can manage your time more effectively, increase productivity, and create a structured routine that keeps you on track with your goals.

As I became more comfortable with the process, I began delegating responsibilities to relevant team members, setting clear timelines, and reviewing progress weekly to ensure we stayed on course. This structured approach made navigating the complexities of educational funding more manageable and laid the foundation for our success.

The first funding stream I focused on was apprenticeships. By partnering with experienced training providers already well-versed in the necessary paperwork, I built a thriving cohort of learners while ensuring full compliance with regulations. This initial step laid the foundation for our entire funding journey and allowed us to learn all the compliance paperwork. As a result, when we later pursued our contracts, we could mirror these processes seamlessly. This experience taught us a valuable lesson: do not try to run before you can walk. Focus on doing one thing at a time, get it right, and then move on. Although apprenticeships are among the most complex funding streams, they turned out to be surprisingly accessible, offering us critical insights that would guide our future efforts.

One of the key advantages of partnering with established training providers was the training they offered, often for a nominal fee. This support helped us implement systems and processes to maintain compliance without feeling overwhelmed. I would strongly recommend working with a consultant or mentor to help navigate these processes and ensure quality. The consequences of non-compliance can be severe, as the Education and Skills Funding Agency will reclaim funds if you fail to meet their stringent requirements. I hope this chapter will fill you with confidence, helping you understand what is available and how it can fit into your business model.

Throughout my career, I've tapped into various funding streams, such as apprenticeship funding, adult education budgets, study programmes, advanced loans, local and county council grants and interest-free business loans directly from the government. Each funding type brought its own challenges and lessons. For instance, securing over £100,000 from council grants in one year was a highlight, proving the potential of well-crafted proposals.

As I share these insights, we're currently in the process of securing another significant funding pot of £100,000. Initially, we considered stepping away from this opportunity because the project we had planned to use the funds for had changed. However, our proposal was so well-crafted, with a strong focus on job creation in the local area, that the funders asked us to tweak it for another project—expanding our Tonbridge site to make it bigger. This adjustment aligns perfectly with the funders' goals, as it will create more jobs, not only by employing additional trainers but also by teaching hair services and business growth strategies to unemployed individuals. This experience highlights the importance of tailoring your bid to meet the funder's priorities, increasing your chances of success.

I approach all our bids like a sales proposal, which helps me communicate effectively. Typically, we are addressing one person, not a group, and I want them to understand that they will achieve their desired results by working with us. Remember: many of these people have been given a budget to spend and need you to utilise it effectively.

Note of warning: you must be ready to adapt to changes and explore new horizons, as the funding landscape is always evolving. For example, when the Wolf Report led to a shift from NVQs to new Apprenticeship Standards in 2018, it required quick adaptation to keep funding streams. This dynamic environment pushed me to diversify our offerings and explore private funding, European Social Funding schemes and traineeship funding. This not only secured our business's future but enhanced its value for a potential exit strategy.

Adaptability and a willingness to explore new opportunities are key to thriving in this ever-changing field. Many training providers are selective about the types of government funding they pursue, often overlooking the strategic advantage of diversifying funding sources. This approach is critically flawed for several reasons:

Relying on a single funding stream makes a business vulnerable to policy shifts and funding cuts. History has shown that government policies can change swiftly, and without a diversified funding base, the stability of a training provider can be compromised. For example, as I scale my business and set up satellite centres around the country, I have noticed that many trainers previously used to access advanced loans. However, with new rules, including the requirement to hold a Grade 2 Ofsted rating, they have lost funding because the providers they worked with failed to set them up properly. This is why any satellite we set up delivers the same quality of training we do. Remember, diversifying your funding sources is crucial for stability.

By leveraging multiple funding streams, training providers can enhance their resilience and adaptability, facilitating sustainable growth over time. This strategy not only safeguards the business financially but broadens the scope of potential training programmes and services that can be offered.

Throughout the chapter, I have included useful links and resources to guide you through the initial steps and beyond, whether you're setting up as a new provider or scaling an existing operation. By sharing my experiences and the lessons I've learned, I hope to make your journey smoother and more manageable. Adaptability and a willingness to explore new opportunities are key to thriving in this ever-changing field.

For those who prefer a more guided experience, I'm here to help. I offer workshops, courses and in-person days to handhold you through every step of the process. My aim is to help you achieve positive outcomes in your funding endeavours.

Understanding the Various Funding Options:

Apprenticeship Funding: This is the most reliable source, consistently available and, as of my last update in 2024, not subject to caps. The only significant challenge came after the Wolf Report, which led to a shift from NVQs to the new Apprenticeship Standards. These standards, created by employers for employers, have set a new benchmark in training quality in England.

For example, at That Nail Place Ltd., my salon business, we contributed to developing the beauty standard. One notable advancement with these new standards is that trainees must be industry-ready upon completion. The standards are tiered (distinction, merit, pass, or fail), which helps employers evaluate candidates based on the effort and skills they have demonstrated during their apprenticeship.

Becoming an Apprenticeship Provider:

If you're considering delivering an apprenticeship, your first step should be to visit the Institute for Apprenticeships website and search for standards relevant to your field. If you can't find a suitable standard, you can team up with other employers to develop a new one. This collaborative process has been successful in fields as diverse as space exploration and robotics. It involves creating a curriculum that meets specific industry needs and designing a rigorous end-point assessment to maintain high standards. By doing this, you ensure the training is top-notch and industry-ready.

There are three main types of apprenticeship providers:

1. **Primary Providers:** Engage directly with employers, using the apprenticeship service for funding, or hold a contract with the Department for Education (DfE).
2. **Employer Providers:** Provide training for their own staff or affiliated companies.
3. **Supporting Providers:** Work under subcontract with primary or employer providers to enhance the training offered.

Starting as a supporting provider, I gradually built our capability from 2008 to 2020. When we were confident in our quality and retention rates - key metrics monitored by the ESFA - we expanded our role and applied to join the Apprenticeship Provider and Assessment Register (APAR).

Who Can Be Trained Using Apprenticeship Funding?

Apprenticeships are a fantastic way to combine practical work experience with academic study, offering a real-world learning environment that's different from traditional education. They are available to anyone over sixteen who isn't in full-time education and lives in England. Apprenticeships range from Level 2 (equivalent to GCSEs) up to Level 7 (equivalent to a master's degree), with durations varying based on the level and the apprentice's prior experience.

Apprentices are compensated based on their age, the stage of their apprenticeship and minimum wage laws. There is also some extra help available: apprentices aged sixteen to twenty-four who are in care or have recently left care may be eligible for a £3,000 bursary. Employers who hire 16-18-year-olds and have fewer than fifty employees can receive a grant to help with wage costs. For apprentices aged 16-22, the apprenticeship is fully funded. If the apprentice is twenty-three or older, the employer only needs to pay a 5% contribution. Do not let this put you off. For example, a £10,000 course would only cost the employer £500.

Plus, if an employer pays the apprenticeship levy, this contribution is taken as a tax. Many large employers pass on this benefit to smaller employers so it doesn't go to waste. This way, everyone can take advantage of the funding available.

For me, I started as a supporting provider and, after building up my numbers from 2008 to 2020, I felt confident in what I was doing. When the apprenticeship register opened, I applied for my own contract and it was approved. We were finally able to grow independently.

Has it been easy? Not at all. There were times I wondered if it was worth it, but we stuck with it. I truly believe that before rolling out to a large audience, it's crucial to trial a small cohort first: say, ten to thirty trainees. Getting regular feedback from these trainees and their employers ensures you can demonstrate and sustain not only the quality but the retention of your trainees, which is heavily measured by the ESFA.

Once you're confident that the course is fit for purpose and up to a standard you're proud of, you can start increasing the number of people on these programmes and then grow your provision. Later, in the Dream Team, part of this book, I'll cover the qualifications and experience your team will need to deliver this training and how to access funding to support this.

Adult Education Budget Funding

When I started delivering apprenticeships, one of my biggest challenges was offering training to low-income students, often single mums or young adults aged nineteen to twenty-five, working part-time in retail or care jobs, or unemployed but aspiring to gain skilled qualifications. Over time, I've taught digital skills, maths, English and hair and nail programmes using various funding sources. The Adult Education Budget (AEB) funding, managed by the Education and Skills Funding Agency (ESFA), has been a vital resource in this journey.

It aims to equip adults with the skills needed for employment, apprenticeships or further education in England.

Key Aspects of AEB Funding

Eligibility and Allocation:

The Adult Education Budget (AEB) is designed for learners aged nineteen and over, and training providers receive funding based on their ability to deliver high-quality education that aligns with local labour market needs. To secure a direct contract, providers must apply for AEB funding through the ESFA's annual contracting process. However, many colleges will subcontract this funding if they are underspending, which is a common occurrence. Before we won our direct contract, this is how we delivered our first courses—by utilizing this subcontracted funding. Even now, if we spend our allocated funds early, we still tender for other bids with colleges to continue delivering courses using this money.

Purpose and Use:

This funding supports a wide range of programmes, including basic maths and English, digital skills training, vocational training and community learning. It is designed to help unemployed individuals or those in low-skilled jobs to improve their employability and skills.

Flexibility in Delivery:

AEB funding is flexible, allowing training providers to tailor programmes to adult learners' needs with options like flexible scheduling and various delivery methods, including online, in-person or blended learning.

To continue receiving AEB funding, providers must show good performance in learner outcomes and progression, ensuring training leads to positive destinations such as employment or further education.

Partnership and Collaboration:

For businesses interested in accessing AEB funding for training, it's essential to understand your local areas by researching skills gaps and educational needs within the local community or region to design programmes aligned with local economic strategies and employer requirements.

Working with local businesses, community groups, and other educational institutions enhances the relevance and impact of training programs. This collaboration ensures that the skills taught align with current labour market demands and lead to direct employment opportunities for graduates. We actively engage with local job centres, Mums groups, and community leaders, who often refer potential clients to us for training. A small gesture like bringing a plate of donuts when visiting the local Jobcentre Plus (JCP) has always worked for me—JCP advisors remember us, and it helps build a positive relationship. Remember, you're helping them achieve one of their main outcomes: placing people in jobs. Being kind and building these connections not only strengthens our programs but also improves our chances of securing funding, as we can demonstrate this community engagement in our bids.

You will need to demonstrate capability by showing that you have the infrastructure, capability and track record to deliver high-quality education and training. This includes having qualified staff, appropriate facilities and a robust learner support system.

You will need to apply through the Education Skills Funding Agency *and* follow the application and contracting processes. This involves a detailed proposal outlining how the funds will be used, programme delivery methods and outcome measurements, such as progression into employment or further education. Typically, this is done through a tendering process. To make the process quicker, I recommend engaging an expert in this field, who normally will be a bid writer or funding consultant. When we started, we partnered with colleges or training providers looking for partners or subcontractors to help build our numbers and gain experience. This was one of the many factors that helped when we bid for our first direct contract; we were successful in February 2023.

By successfully securing AEB funding, you can expand your training offerings to cater to a broader adult learner base, significantly contributing to the community by enhancing adults' skills and employability. This support benefits not only the learners but the local economy by creating a more skilled workforce.

Our Comprehensive Training Programmes

What we did—and you could do similarly in your area of expertise—was develop a range of programmes tailored for hair, beauty and nail technicians, equipping them with essential skills for success. Our programmes go beyond technical training to include digital literacy, helping participants grow their client base through social media, and business skills such as drafting business plans, job application preparation and interview skills.

Additionally, we incorporate retail training to enhance their ability to upsell products and services. We prioritise holistic development by organising wellness days that address mental health and mindset. Community engagement is also encouraged, with participants offering their services in local elderly homes and operating a training salon that provides affordable treatments to those who might not otherwise afford them.

To bridge the gap between training and employment, we host employer interview days, allowing local businesses to scout for potential apprentices or part-time employees among our students. This initiative helps students gain valuable work experience, aids their transition into the workforce or further education and supports some in starting their own service businesses.

Starting as a subcontractor to an established, funded training provider allowed us to build a successful track record while learning the compliance requirements and relevant paperwork, all with the support of the lead funding provider. This experience positioned us to secure independent funding through successful tenders. I highly recommend this approach, as it saves you much time. Once you secure your financing, you can mirror their processes and systems, which further enhances your efficiency. This strategy not only strengthens your training programs but also significantly contributes to the personal and professional growth of your team and the clients you serve.

What is Study Programme Funding?

In 2013, we secured our first study funding contract for 16-18-year-olds by partnering with another private training provider. This partnership came after we had successfully delivered apprenticeships, which they needed to offer. One of our biggest challenges was finding young people ready for the world of work, as many lacked essential employability soft skills like communication and confidence. They didn't want to return to school or full-time college, so we created a programme that combined learning with a couple of days of work experience. This approach helped them gain these crucial skills and created opportunities for young people transitioning from full-time education into adulthood.

Overcoming Challenges in Securing Funding

Securing this funding is often challenging, as it's typically reserved for specific regions or counties and dominated by FE colleges. Despite the financial rewards being high for short programme durations, the intensive resources required to support young adults facing various insecurities and challenges make it a complex endeavour. However, our experience and dedication have allowed us to overcome these obstacles and make a meaningful impact on the lives of these young individuals.

The Strategy: Filling the Gaps Left by FE Colleges

Early on, we recognised that FE colleges often prioritise students who excel academically in maths and English, leaving behind those not in education or employment. By pitching this idea to local colleges and other training providers not interested in delivering these programmes themselves, we secured additional contracts as a subcontractor. This arrangement allows them to earn a percentage of the funding (30-50%) without doing the work, providing them with clear profit.

These programmes have been a collaborative effort involving local employers who provide critical work experience. Young clients complete work diaries and receive feedback and references from their employers at the programme's conclusion. This practical approach not only equips them with the necessary skills but the confidence to progress to apprenticeships of their choice as they experience different fields of work.

Annually, we have successfully assisted approximately seventy young people through this programme. By the end, 75% have progressed to full-time work, further learning in colleges, or apprenticeships. An additional

20% found employment or started an apprenticeship within twelve months after completing our programme.

How Can You Win these bids?

Identify Gaps: Recognise areas where FE colleges may leave gaps, particularly for students who don't excel academically.

Partner with Providers: Collaborate with local colleges, schools and training providers, offering to deliver these programs on their behalf in exchange for a percentage of the funding.

Incorporate Work Experience: Combine learning with practical work experience to equip young people with essential skills and confidence.

Track and Report Outcomes: Monitor the progress and outcomes of your students to prove the programme's success and secure continued funding.

By implementing these strategies, you can effectively support young people transitioning from full-time education into adulthood, making a meaningful impact on their lives while securing a steady stream of funding for your organisation.

What Are Skills Bootcamps?

Skills Bootcamps in the UK are part of the government's 'Lifetime Skills Guarantee and Plan for Jobs'. These bootcamps offer flexible courses of up to sixteen weeks for individuals aged nineteen and over, providing training in specific skill areas, such as digital, construction and green energy, with a clear route into employment or a new career path. Funding for these bootcamps is designed to enhance the employability of adults and fill skill gaps in high-demand sectors.

Skills Bootcamp Funding

As we explore new avenues to expand our training services, Skills Bootcamps have emerged as a promising opportunity that we are eager to incorporate into our offerings. While we haven't yet ventured into Skills Bootcamps, we are thoroughly preparing and strategically planning for this new initiative. Currently, we are collaborating with a bid writer and education strategist to explore how we can integrate this initiative into our existing suite of training services.

Our Approach and Recommendations

Skills Bootcamps are designed to quickly equip adults aged nineteen and over with the skills needed in sectors experiencing shortages. These bootcamps are ideal for individuals looking to advance in their current roles, switch careers or re-enter the workforce. Developed in partnership with employers, education providers and local authorities, these programmes ensure that the training is practical and relevant.

Predominantly funded in England by the Department for Education (DfE), securing funding for these bootcamps requires providers to submit competitive bids or respond to allocated funding calls. Often, there is an expectation of co-investment from employers, especially when the training is tailored to meet specific corporate needs or when participants are guaranteed interviews post-training.

During our preparation phase, staying informed about upcoming funding calls from the DfE is crucial. This allows us to position ourselves advantageously to submit compelling bids that showcase our ability to deliver impactful training aligned with regional skills gaps. Designing courses that meet these gaps and collaborating with local employers are key to ensuring the success and sustainability of our bootcamps.

Implementing robust tracking and reporting systems to monitor participant success and employment outcomes is essential. Maintaining high standards of training and providing ongoing support for learners are crucial to preserve the credibility and effectiveness of our bootcamps, ensuring continued funding and success.

For those considering launching Skills Bootcamps, it's advisable to gain experience in similar educational initiatives first. This approach helps in understanding the operational and educational frameworks necessary to succeed. Engaging in detailed planning and consultations with industry partners can significantly enhance the relevance and impact of the training provided.

By methodically preparing to introduce Skills Bootcamps into our training portfolio, we aim to extend our educational services and effectively address the skill shortages in our community. This initiative, while challenging, aligns perfectly with our commitment to excellence and our core value of 'Commitment to Success'.

Unlocking Opportunities with Advanced Learner Loans

Advanced Learner Loans are a powerful tool to make further education more accessible for adults aged nineteen and over. Similar to university loans, these loans cover the upfront costs of training for those aspiring to pursue Level 3 to Level 6 qualifications. Managed by the Student Loans Company, these loans have allowed us to extend our training programs to include higher-level courses such as salon management, microblading and advanced techniques in hair and nails.

How We Have Utilised Advanced Learner Loans

To access Advanced Learner Loans directly, an educational provider must be a lead provider and maintain at least a Grade 2 Ofsted rating. However, we've effectively collaborated with lead providers, offering our specialised training under their umbrella and receiving compensation in return. This partnership has expanded our reach and supported our growth.

For learners who might not qualify for traditional funding or those looking to progress from Level 2 qualifications, Advanced Learner Loans are ideal. The repayment terms are income-contingent and begin only once the learner earns above a certain threshold, making it a familiar and manageable system. Our trainers have successfully incorporated Levels 4 and 5 qualifications, broadening their professional scope and the skills they can pass on to learners.

How You Can Benefit

By leveraging Advanced Learner Loans, you can expand your training offerings to include higher-level courses. This financial model eases the burden for learners, opening up opportunities for those who might otherwise be unable to afford further education. Highlighting the availability of these loans in your marketing can make your programmes more attractive and accessible.

Assisting learners throughout the application process and providing continuous support once they are enrolled can ensure they complete their courses successfully. This approach improves course completion rates and overall satisfaction, demonstrating your commitment to their success.

Implementing Advanced Learner Loans

Collaboration: Partner with lead providers to offer specialised training under their umbrella.

Course Expansion: Use the loans to develop and offer higher-level courses.

Marketing: Highlight the loans' availability to attract more learners.

Support: Help learners with the application process and provide ongoing support.

Integrating Advanced Learner Loans into your funding strategy can enhance your educational offerings and fill skill gaps in the workforce. By following our approach, you can expand your reach, support your growth and make a significant impact on your learners' lives.

This funding model has allowed us to remain at the forefront of vocational training, and it can do the same for you.

Leveraging Council Funding for Growth

Over the years, understanding and utilising council grants has become a cornerstone of our strategy for enhancing our training provisions. These grants have provided substantial support, from improving our facilities to offering introductory taster courses. For example, our recent engagement with the Multiply funding initiative, launched by the government post-Brexit, has been a game-changer. In 2024, we've used this programme to offer online basic skills courses like maths, which teach practical skills such as pricing services and include short, hands-on sessions in basic hair and beauty skills over three days. This approach builds confidence among new learners, grows relationships and eases them into the learning environment without overwhelming them.

How We Have Utilised Council Funding

Council funding has been instrumental in upgrading our infrastructure. For instance, we completely refitted our training salon, installing new doors, sinks and workstations. These improvements have directly contributed to a better learning environment and, by extension, more effective training outcomes.

How You Can Access and Maximise Council Grants

Align with Council Goals: Each council has its own strategic goals and priorities. Part of our success has come from aligning our projects with these objectives, ensuring we meet community needs and are seen as valuable partners by local authorities.

Engage with Council Members: Building relationships with council members and economic development officers has been crucial for our success. These connections provide valuable insights into council funding priorities and keep us informed about upcoming grant opportunities. Thanks to these strong relationships, we often receive emails from council officials and administration teams when new funding becomes available, as they know we deliver results. Remember: it's all about building relationships and ensuring a win-win for all parties involved

Prepare Strong Applications: Our applications detail how our projects will positively impact the local community. We outline objectives, expected impacts, clear budgets and timelines. Including evidence of past successes strengthens our proposals significantly.

Collaborate with Local Organisations: Partnering with other local organisations enhances our applications. These collaborations show community-wide support and resource pooling, which is highly favourable in the eyes of council grant committees.

Monitor and Report Progress: Once funding is secured, it is crucial to diligently monitor and report on progress. Detailed reporting maintains transparency with the council and proves that funds are used as intended to achieve meaningful community impacts.

Research Local Opportunities: Depending on your location, available funding may vary. For example, you can explore Kent County Council's community grants and funding page for opportunities. Simply replace "Kent" with your local county to find grants in your area.

Kent County Council Community Grants and Funding

Conclusion

Council funding has enabled us to improve our facilities and expand our offerings: it has played a pivotal role in our strategic growth. By effectively leveraging these grants, we have enhanced our ability to serve our community better and have laid a strong foundation for continual growth and success in the training sector. This proactive approach to utilising council grants exemplifies our commitment to 'Going Above and Beyond' as standard, ensuring we provide top-tier training and support to our learners.

Chapter 5

Finding & Tendering for Contracts

So, how do you tender for government contracts? This involves several steps. I have tried to break this down as a step-by-step guide to help you navigate the process:

1. Find Contract Opportunities

- **Education & Training**: This is the main portal for finding tenders in the education sector. **https://education.bravosolution.co.uk/web/login.shtml**

- **Contracts Finder:** This is the main portal for finding public sector contracts above £10,000 in central government and £25,000 in the wider public sector.
https://www.contractsfinder.service.gov.uk/Search
- **TED (Tenders Electronic Daily):** The online version of the 'Supplement to the Official Journal' of the EU, dedicated to European public procurement.
https://ted.europa.eu/en/
- **Find a Tender (FTS):** For notices above the thresholds set out in the Public Contracts Regulations 2015. Find a Tender:
https://www.gov.uk/find-tender
- **Bid Stats**: This is a fast and easy **tender** search and is free. You search by keyword, region or notice type. There is no registration required.
https://bidstats.uk/tenders/search
- **Ministry of Justice:** This is for prisons. We have only bid once on this site and were not successful due to location and the amount we wanted per learner. We will bid there again, no doubt, and it is worth taking a look at.
https://www.gov.uk/government/organisations/ministry-of-justice/about/procurement

- **Procurement at DWP (Department for Work and Pensions):** This is the site of the Department of Work and Pensions and relates to job centre's bids and other types of bids for the unemployed. They also have a small provision for smaller businesses. **https://www.gov.uk/government/organisations/department-for-work-pensions/about/procurement**

2. Register Your Business

- The next step is to register on relevant portals like Contracts Finder, TED and other sector-specific portals.
- Make sure that you keep your company details up to date on these platforms, particularly your email address, where you are located and the bids you are interested in.

3. Prepare Your Business

- **Understand the Requirements:** It is important to read the tender documents carefully to understand the requirements, criteria and processes so you can not only plan your time but ensure you fit the requirements and have the ability to deliver what they are asking for.
- **Assess Your Suitability:** Please make sure your business meets the contract requirements. Consider the financial, technical and resource implications for your business, such as staff costs, having a team in place, and having the venue to

deliver the required training and the cash flow to sustain your current business if your payments are delayed for any reason.

- **Certifications and Standards:** Ensure you have necessary certifications (e.g., ISO standards, Cyber Essentials) as required by the tender. I will cover these under policies and procedures and the accreditation chapters.

4. Expression of Interest (EOI)

- Submit an EOI if required. This step may include completing a pre-qualification questionnaire (PQQ).

5. Pre-Qualification Questionnaire (PQQ)

- The PQQ assesses your capability and capacity to undertake the contract.
- Start preparing the documents that demonstrate your experience, financial stability and technical abilities.
- You will need to provide evidence of past performance and relevant case studies. Make sure these are true reflections, as they *will* check. This is why we often work with other providers at the beginning to gain this evidence.
- You will then need to keep your eye out for updates on the tender. There is often a delay before you hear back.

6. Invitation to Tender (ITT)

- If you pass the PQQ stage, you will then receive an ITT.
- The ITT document will include detailed specifications, terms and conditions, and the evaluation criteria. Remember, if you are not successful the first time, use it as a learning process. In our first few tenders, we did not win, but we learnt from each one and we implemented our learnings.

7. Writing the Tender

Writing a successful bid for a tender in the education sector requires careful planning, a deep understanding of the tender requirements, and a clear demonstration of your organisation's capabilities. Here's a step-by-step guide on what to consider:

Understand the Tender Requirements

- **Read the Tender Document Thoroughly**: Ensure you fully understand the scope, objectives, and specific requirements of the tender. Note any mandatory criteria, deadlines, and submission formats.
- **Clarify Any Doubts**: If anything is unclear, seek clarification from the issuing authority before the deadline for queries.

Research and Analysis

- **Understand the Client's Needs**: Research the organisation issuing the tender, their goals, and challenges in education. Tailor your bid to address their specific needs.
- **Analyse the Competition**: Consider who your competitors might be and how you can differentiate your bid by offering superior value or unique expertise.

Tailor Your Proposal

- **Align with the Objectives**: Ensure your proposal clearly aligns with the tender objectives, demonstrating how your approach meets or exceeds the expectations.
- **Use Relevant Experience**: Highlight previous experience in similar projects, focusing on successful outcomes, and how this experience makes you the best candidate.
- **Showcase Expertise**: Demonstrate your team's qualifications, expertise, and capability to deliver the project on time and within budget.

Structure Your Bid

- **Executive Summary**: Provide a concise overview of your proposal, summarising how you intend to meet the tender's objectives and why your organisation is best suited for the project.
- **Project Plan**: Include a detailed plan outlining your approach, methodology, timelines, and deliverables. Ensure the plan is realistic and achievable.
- **Compliance and Quality Assurance**: Detail how you will comply with all regulatory and quality standards, particularly if they are specific to education.
- **Risk Management**: Identify potential risks and explain how you will mitigate them, ensuring the client that you have a proactive and reliable approach.
- **Budget and Pricing**: Offer a transparent and competitive pricing structure. Justify your costs with a breakdown and ensure it reflects value for money.
- **Value Added**: Highlight any additional value your proposal brings, such as innovative approaches, additional services, or long-term benefits to the client.

Presentation and Clarity

- **Clear and Concise Language**: Write in a clear, professional, and concise manner. Avoid jargon and ensure the bid is easy to read and understand.
- **Professional Layout**: Use a well-organised layout with headings, subheadings, bullet points, and graphics (if applicable) to make the document visually appealing and easy to navigate.
- **Proofread**: Thoroughly proofread your bid to avoid any errors or inconsistencies. A well-polished document reflects professionalism and attention to detail. You can use a bid writer for this as they will often give you helpful feedback for a lesser fee than if they had to write the bid themselves.

Compliance and Submission

- **Follow Instructions**: Adhere strictly to the tender instructions, including format, length, and submission process. Non-compliance can result in disqualification.
- **Submit on Time**: Ensure your bid is submitted well before the deadline to avoid last-minute issues. Confirm the receipt of your submission with the issuing authority.

Post-Submission

- **Be Ready for Clarifications**: Be prepared to provide additional information or clarifications if requested by the tendering body.
- **Learn from Feedback**: If your bid is unsuccessful, request feedback to understand areas for improvement in future bids.
- **Presentations:** Sometimes, you will be asked to present your proposal.

Award Notification

- If successful, you will receive an award notification.
- If unsuccessful, always seek feedback to improve your future tenders.

Contract Management

- **Deliver as Promised:** Ensure you deliver the contract as per the agreed terms.
- **Maintain Communication:** Keep lines of communication open with the contracting authority.
- **Monitor Performance:** Regularly monitor and report on your performance.

Additional Tips:

- **Networking:** Attend relevant industry and government networking events.
- **Consortiums:** If the contract is too large, consider forming a consortium with other businesses.
- **Staying Updated:** Make sure you keep abreast of changes in public procurement regulations and practices.
- **Focus on the Client's Needs:** Your bid should clearly reflect how you will meet the client's needs better than your competitors.
- **Innovation and Best Practices:** Showcase how your approach incorporates innovative solutions and best practices in education.
- **Team Credentials:** Highlight the qualifications and experience of your team, emphasising their ability to deliver high-quality education services.
- **Provide Evidence:** Use case studies, references and metrics to support your claims. Once again, you can produce this by working with other providers as a partner so you can demonstrate your achievements and outcomes.
- **Be Clear and Concise:** When you are passionate about your business, you can often go off on a tangent (I often do), so having someone like a bid writer overseeing it will help you stay on point.
- **Pricing:** Provide a competitive and realistic pricing model. Again, justify your costs as these need to be believable. We did when we tendered for our

council grant; we received several quotes, as well as having our staff costs looked at. These bids will often only pay 50% towards your project (yet 50% really helped us make the changes we needed to our building).

- **Networking:** Attend relevant industry and government networking events.
- **Consortiums:** If the contract is too large, consider forming a consortium with other businesses.
- **Staying Updated:** Make sure you keep abreast of changes in public procurement regulations and practices.

By following these steps and thoroughly preparing your business, you can effectively compete for and win government contracts in the UK.

Chapter 6

Maximising Funding Opportunities: A Strategic Overview

On our journey to develop and expand our training offerings, we've learned to navigate the complex landscape of funding sources. From apprenticeships and study programmes to adult education funding, Advanced Learner Loans and Skills Bootcamps, each funding stream has played a crucial role in our ability to provide comprehensive and accessible training. Here is how we've strategically engaged with these opportunities:

Building Strategic Partnerships

The cornerstone of our strategy has been building and maintaining strong relationships with key stakeholders across various funding bodies, including local job centres, the Department for Work and Pensions (DWP) and even the Ministry of Defence & local councils. Engaging actively on platforms like LinkedIn, interacting with posts and directly reaching out to senior managers has been instrumental. Being part of associations like the Kent Association of Training Organisations (KATO) has opened doors to extensive networks and resources. Face-to-face relationships build trust: this has helped us be on funders' radars when they are looking for partners, so I would highly recommend you do the same.

Utilising Local and National Funding Sources

Our approach has been to utilise a mix of local and national funding sources. Each source, whether direct government funding, council grants or sector-specific funds like those for defence, has its criteria and challenges. By understanding these nuances and aligning our programmes accordingly, we have been able to tap into these diverse funds effectively.

Leveraging Funding for Programme Development

We have used funding for basic course provision, enhancing our facilities and introducing innovative programme elements such as taster courses. These initiatives have helped reduce barriers for new learners and have provided them with valuable introductory experiences.

Navigating the Funding Application Process

Knowing how to write a compelling tender has been a critical skill. Initially, we handled this in-house, which not only kept our applications aligned with our mission and values but taught us valuable lessons in storytelling and relevance. As we grew, we invested in retaining a bid writer, streamlining the process and enhancing our capacity to secure and manage larger contracts. I truly believe it's best if you can use a combination of yourself and the bid writer. But remember, if you are not successful with your first few bids, you get feedback. These were great lessons as they helped us to make changes to our bids, and now we are very rarely unsuccessful, as we have learned in more detail what they are looking for.

Engaging with Funding Bodies

Understanding the needs and challenges of funding bodies has enabled us to tailor our offerings to meet their requirements. Whether it's addressing the skills gaps identified by local job centres or designing courses that support military personnel transitioning to civilian roles, our focus has always been on providing solutions to their most pressing problems.

Continuous Learning and Adaptation

Staying proactive about learning how to manage and apply for funding has been crucial. We recommend all potential training providers get involved with tendering websites and training courses on proposal writing. For those looking to bypass the complexities of direct funding management, partnering with established providers like ours offers a viable pathway to deliver impactful training programmes.

Conclusion

By strategically engaging with a variety of funding sources and building robust partnerships, we've been able to offer diverse and impactful educational programmes. This approach has enabled us not only to expand our reach but to contribute significantly to workforce development in our community. Remember: the key to successful funding acquisition lies in understanding the pain points of funding bodies and presenting your training solutions as the answer to their needs.

By following our strategic overview, you too can maximise funding opportunities and make a meaningful impact on your learners and community.

Chapter 7

Accreditation, Regulated and Quality Training and Why it Matters for Funders

When I decided to pursue government funding for our training programmes, I knew having accredited and regulated qualifications was crucial to scale TNB skills training in the long-term.

To secure government funding, it was essential to meet their standards and requirements. Accredited and regulated qualifications were not just a prerequisite but a demonstration of our commitment to quality. By aligning with these standards, we showed the government that we were trustworthy partners.

Having recognised qualifications meant we could build credibility and trust with employers, educational institutions, and stakeholders. The accreditation process has been a game-changer for us. It ensures that our training programmes maintain consistent standards and undergo regular audits. This not only improves the reliability and effectiveness of our training but drives continuous improvement.

With accredited qualifications, your business will gain a competitive edge. It makes you more attractive to potential clients and partners, enhancing your brand reputation as a provider of high-quality, reliable training. I highly recommend this to anyone who wants to be assured they can deliver funded training on behalf of the government and who would love to work with corporations.

Securing government funding will also significantly reduce your operational costs and provide financial stability. This support allows you to focus on improving training quality and expanding your offerings, making resource allocation more efficient.

Accredited & regulated qualifications will open doors to new markets and opportunities. You will be able to collaborate with other educational institutions and businesses and scale your operations to serve more clients.

Clients will have greater confidence in your training programmes because they are backed by recognised qualifications. Additionally, you will attract better talent, both in trainers and trainees, which enhances the overall value proposition of your business.

The combination of government funding and the credibility of accredited & regulated qualifications has contributed to our long-term sustainability and growth. It has allowed us to invest in innovative training methods and technologies, keeping us ahead of industry trends.

Choosing to pursue accredited and regulated qualifications becomes a strategic decision that will pay off immensely. It will ensure compliance with standards, build your credibility, open up funding opportunities and strengthen your market position. This route will lead to increased marketability, financial support, expansion opportunities and long-term sustainability, significantly boosting the overall value of your business.

The difference between accredited and regulated: why it matters when bidding

Let's clear up some confusion today—because I know so many people still don't quite get it, and I promised I'd help you out!

So, who is Ofqual?

Ofqual stands for the Office of Qualifications and Examinations Regulation. This non-ministerial government department in the UK handles regulation of qualifications, exams, and assessments in England. They make sure qualifications are high-quality, standards are consistent, and the exam process is fair and reliable.

Here's the key takeaway: If your certificate does not have Ofqual on it, it is not regulated. That means it is unlikely to be eligible for funded training—not impossible, just unlikely.

Awarding Organisations: Accreditation Approval and Fees

So, how do you become accredited & regulated? To offer accredited and regulated qualifications, you must become an approved centre of the awarding organisation that provides the qualification(s) you wish to deliver. This includes functional skills if you plan to become a provider of apprenticeships or 16-18 study programmes and adult education training.

The process is quite similar across awarding organisations, all of which are regulated in the UK by Ofqual. However, there are slight differences between vocational centre approval and academic centre approval for functional skills or GCSEs.

You'll need to start by applying to the awarding organisation(s) of your choice, which begins with providing some basic company details and undergoing a credit check. You'll also need to supply approximate registration numbers, meaning how many students you predict will enrol and the qualifications you're seeking approval for. If you're like we were, these numbers might be small to begin with, but as we grew, those predictions expanded significantly.

Most awarding organisations charge an approval fee, typically ranging from £1,000 to £2,000. They may also charge a fee if your registration spending is below a certain threshold. For example, VTCT charges an annual fee of around £850 if spending on registrations in the previous year was below £10,000. The amount and point at which this fee is applied varies across awarding organisations. NCFE, for instance, charges an annual fee of £950 regardless of your registration levels.

Qualification registration costs vary, ranging from around £40 for a single unit to £120 to £200 for a full diploma qualification.

End-point assessment (EPA) costs for Apprenticeship Standards vary from around £500 to £1,500 depending on the EPA Organisation, Apprenticeship Standard and components of assessment.

In my experience, it's crucial to factor in these costs and requirements as part of your planning process to ensure smooth approval and ongoing compliance. Many of our clients prefer to stay as a satellite and work under us as a partner because it allows them to operate under our guidance, with us taking the lead. This arrangement often makes things easier for them and ensures everything runs smoothly, as well as saving the cost of registrations. I believe other training providers will do the same.

When we first applied, we used a consultant to help us through the process, which saved us time. The positive thing is that once you have approval from one awarding body, the process for others is really straightforward. We recently introduced a 'done-for-you' service for the businesses we work with, as it can sometimes be overwhelming and time consuming to begin with.

Awarding Organisations: Accreditation Approval

Once you have completed the initial checks, you will need to provide a combination of the following:

- You'll need to provide details about your key personnel, including roles like the head of the centre, an exams officer, a finance contact, and someone in charge of quality. If necessary, the same person can fill multiple roles.
- You'll also need to submit the names, professional profiles or CVs and certificates for your internal quality assurers (IQAs), assessors, and teachers or tutors. The qualifications and experience required for these roles will vary depending on the qualifications you're delivering. Some qualifications have specific requirements for assessor and IQA qualifications, along with a minimum number of years of vocational or professional experience.
- For any qualifications that involve secure live assessment exams, you'll need to show how you meet the requirements for the storage, administration, secure transport, receipt, and handling of assessment materials.
- You'll also need to demonstrate that you have Centre Record Systems in place to effectively track learner progress, achievements, and the recording of exemptions.
- It's crucial to securely store accurate, up-to-date learner details and assessment records. You'll need to keep assessment and IQA records for about three years following certification, although the

exact time frame will be provided by your awarding organisation and any potential funders, who might have different requirements.

- Finally, if the qualifications cannot be delivered online, you must show that you have the physical resources necessary to deliver them. This includes adequate space for practical and theory training, as well as the equipment, tools, products, and resources needed to effectively deliver vocational qualifications. For example, if you're offering hair or beauty qualifications, a working, realistic salon environment is essential.

Additional Requirements for Awarding Organisation Accreditation

In addition to the policies and procedures covered in later chapters, which are essential for government contracts and awarding organisation approvals, awarding organisations may also require the following information and documents:

- **Delivery of Qualifications:** At the accreditation approval stage, you will need to provide a scheme of work and schedule of delivery, demonstrating how guided learning hours and total qualification time will be adequately met. Gaining an award in education and an internal quality assured qualification can help you here, or you can hire someone with these qualifications.

- **Assessment Materials:** You are likely to need examples of assessment materials and assignments.
- **Assessment and Learner Feedback:** Outline how you provide assessment and feedback to learners.
- **Learner Recruitment and Enrolment:** Describe how you recruit and enrol learners, including how you verify their identity and suitability for the qualification, such as meeting entry requirements. You can show this using an application, or consultants can again help with this if it's new to you.
- **Registration, Certification and Withdrawals:** Detail your processes for timely learner registration, certification and handling withdrawals. Things to consider: who can you hire in your team to do this?
- **Recognition of Prior Learning (RPL):** Explain your approach to recognising prior learning. Again, you or a member of your team will learn this on the Award in Education & Assessing qualifications—and guess what? These can be fully funded through the apprenticeship schemes.

Once you have completed the application forms and provided all the required information, you will undergo a virtual or face-to-face centre approval visit with a representative of the awarding organisation. They will visually inspect your facilities to ensure they meet the requirements of the organisation and the qualification(s). Additionally, they will meet with your staff and review the evidence to decide if you should be granted centre approval.

For a clear idea of general requirements, I have included an example of one of our awarding bodies. You can refer to the VTCT approval criteria document link:

https://www.vtct.org.uk/wp-content/uploads/2021/09/Approval-Visit-Criteria_v9-July-2023.pdf

Functional Skills

Functional skills registrations are normally in the region of £30 per subject. In addition, you will need to purchase software licences for both maths and English to use an initial assessment and diagnostic tool to record starting levels for learners at enrolment.

Sometimes, the licence will also cover the Individual Skills Plan (ISP) for each learner, or there may be an additional charge for this service. You will need the ISP to provide your learner with an individualised learning tool for each functional skill, as this software will provide the learning resources for each subject area identified in their diagnostic assessment that need to be developed to pass the exam at Level 1 or Level 2. We use a company called 'NCFE skills forward' but there are other companies out there and I recommend you do some research.

You will also need to provide teaching for your learners to support their online ISP, either with your vocational teachers, if they are able, or with a dedicated maths and/or English tutor. Apprentices who have not already achieved GCSE Grades 4-9 or A*-C must pass functional skills in maths and English at either Level 1 or Level 2, depending on the level of apprenticeship they are undertaking. They cannot enter Gateway for End Point Assessment until they have achieved their maths and English passes as part of the apprenticeship schemes, so if you are going to deliver these, please consider this in your costings.

Qualification and CPD (Continuous Professional Development) Requirements

Centres must ensure that unqualified assessors and IQAs are registered on an appropriate qualification and have an action plan and time for completion, usually within twelve months. Centres must ensure that all decisions made by unqualified assessors or IQAs are countersigned by a qualified and competent assessor or IQA, respectively.

Unless otherwise specified in a qualification's assessment strategy or specification, assessors must be competent and hold at least one recognised, regulated assessing qualification to be considered a qualified assessor.

IQAs must be competent and hold at least a recognised, regulated, internal verification/quality assurance qualification to be considered a qualified IQA. Please note that IQAs may only quality assure evidence that they did not themselves assess.

N.B. Teaching staff are deemed competent if they hold the same, equivalent or a related higher-level regulated qualification as the qualification or unit they are delivering. Assessing staff and the quality assurance team do not necessarily need to be part of the teaching/delivery team, yet must still meet this requirement. Centres must also have an appropriate number of invigilators for qualifications requiring external assessment under exam conditions.

How we Evidence Qualification and Continuing Personal Development Requirements

Our core value of Passion for Learning is woven throughout everything we do. Assessors and IQAs must engage in CPD (Continuing Professional Development) activities to stay current with developments relevant to the qualifications and units they oversee. CPD is documented through a personal development plan (PDP) or a reflective diary. While CPD is the responsibility of the individual, not the organisation, you will need to show CPD records for your staff during each External Quality visit from your awarding organisation. If you're delivering funded training, either directly or as a subcontractor, Ofsted will expect to see this as part of their framework, so it's crucial to ensure it's followed. We manage this through written training plans, which we revisit during monthly one-to-one meetings and annual appraisals.

CPD requirements may be outlined in the awarding bodies' assessment strategies or qualification specifications. However, if they're not, or if those documents aren't available, you should refer to the sector-specific requirements most awarding organisations set for CPD.

For NVQ Qualification Delivery:

Our awarding bodies ask for a minimum of thirty hours of CPD each year. For new assessors and IQAs, those hours start when they begin their role—there is no pro-rata system for part-time staff. You can count CPD through hands-on work, like taking part in commercial services that help you build your skills or knowledge, and just keep a reflective diary as evidence. Any occupational or technical training that helps you with the qualifications you're assessing or IQA-ing also counts toward your CPD hours.

For Apprenticeship Standard Qualification Delivery:

If you're delivering apprenticeships, our awarding body expects a minimum of fifty hours of CPD each year. No pro-rata for part-time staff. Out of those fifty hours, thirty should be practical skills gained in a commercial setting. The remaining twenty hours can come from a mix of activities—like standardisation meetings, updating your knowledge or skills through the internet, TV, or other media, doing industrial updates through visits, placements, or shadowing, and attending briefings by awarding bodies or colleagues. Again, you can track this CPD through a personal development plan (PDP) or a reflective diary.

Qualification and CPD Requirements

For VRQ Qualification Delivery:

Minimum requirement of thirty hours CPD per annum. The CPD requirements are calculated pro-rata for part-time staff or for staff teaching across subject areas. 70% of these hours are made up of hands-on delivery of relevant services to fee-paying clients in a commercial salon, which can be shown to develop individual skills and knowledge levels, or undertaking technical training that develops new skills and updates existing ones and/or knowledge levels. A further 30% of hours can be evidenced by a range of other activities, including shadowing, standardisation meetings, updating knowledge or skills though the internet, television and other media, industrial updating through visits, placements or shadowing, attending briefings by awarding bodies and colleagues, reading the trade press and books, listening to recordings (such as podcasts and webinars) and watching DVDs, YouTube and social media.

For assessors and IQAs working across subject areas, such as hair and beauty, then the CPD requirements are per subject area and in some cases can be pro-rata, but you must always check your specific awarding organisation requirements.

Some awarding organisations are moving towards a requirement for certificates to be upgraded to accredited qualifications as part of CPD requirements. For example, if you hold a non-accredited ABT or Beauty Guild certificate, you may need to upgrade to a single-unit award from an accredited awarding organisation. Again, you should check individual requirements with your awarding organisation and/or EQA.

What is the difference between VRQ & NVQ qualifications?

A lot of people don't understand the difference between a VRQ and an NVQ, but it's really important to know, especially when it comes to funding, as the funding can differ between the two. VRQs (Vocationally Related Qualifications) are more classroom-based and focus on providing the knowledge and skills needed for a specific job or industry. They're assessed through a mix of assignments, tests, and practical tasks. On the other hand, NVQs (National Vocational Qualifications) are all about practical, on-the-job performance. They require real work experience, and they are assessed by observing you in your actual job role. The key difference is that, while VRQs are more flexible and theory-based, NVQs are rooted in workplace competency. Understanding this distinction is crucial because it can impact the type of funding you're eligible for and how you plan your training programs.

Standardisation Requirements

Standardisation is crucial for ensuring that everyone on your training team is on the same page when it comes to marking and grading. It makes sure that the awarding of competence or grades is clear, consistent, and in line with the awarding organisation's learning outcomes.

This means that, no matter which assessor or tutor a learner has, they're marked fairly against the same assessment criteria.

In our practice, we hold standardisation meetings every two months, where we go through cross-marking exercises to make sure everyone agrees on the expectations and standards. For example, when it comes to the English functional skills speaking and listening module, which often requires audio or video evidence, we listen to an assessment together during these meetings. Then, we all mark the candidates against the subject content statements to ensure everyone would award the same pass grade. If there's any confusion, we clarify it on the spot so that the whole team is aligned.

Standardisation is also important for making sure everyone is familiar with the marking standards and conventions, not just for grading but also for providing feedback. This enables the team to work together smoothly, offering a consistent and fair service to all learners. We also standardise paperwork like learner progress reviews, off-the-job training forms, and additional support provided to learners, including pastoral care.

We document these meetings in minutes, which we distribute to anyone who couldn't attend, so everyone stays in the loop. Awarding organisations will ask for these minutes during their external quality assurance visits to make sure we're staying on top of standardisation and that our assessment marking processes are consistent across the board. This regular practice helps us maintain high standards and ensure that our learners are getting the best, most equitable experience possible.

IQA Sampling and Observations

Internal Quality Assurance (IQA) is a critical process that ensures the assessment of learners is conducted consistently, fairly, and to the required standards. It involves a thorough review and sampling of assessor work, including learner portfolios, reviews, off-the-job training, and any additional support provided for learners with Additional Learning Needs (ALN). The main goal of IQA is to maintain the integrity of the assessment process and to ensure that every learner receives a fair and accurate assessment, regardless of who the assessor is.

IQA sampling takes two key forms:

- **Portfolio and Paperwork Checking**: This confirms that the written and theory work meets the acceptable standards.
- **Direct Observation of Assessors**: During practical assessments, the IQA observes the assessor to ensure they are diligently evaluating the learner's practical skills without being intrusive. The IQA checks that the assessor makes the correct judgement of competence or non-competence based on the assessment criteria. After the assessment, the IQA also observes how the assessor provides constructive feedback to the learner. The IQA then gives their feedback to the

assessor, highlighting best practices and areas for development. This is also a great time for the IQA to interview learners and gather feedback on their learning experience.

Your IQA strategy should consider a range of factors, such as the assessor's experience, length of service with your organisation, workload, number and level of qualifications delivered, and previous sampling feedback. For instance, a new assessor who has just completed training should have 100% of their learner portfolios sampled for their first ten learners. Based on the feedback and any necessary actions, you might reduce the sample size for future learners, but must ensure that every unit of a qualification is sampled at least once.

It's also important to note that assessors in training must have all their work checked and counter-assessed by a qualified assessor before the IQA sampling and checks occur.

If you're new to this process or considering doing IQA yourself, the books by Anne Gravells on Amazon are an excellent resource. They provide a deep understanding of assessing and IQA qualifications and are invaluable, whether you are planning to handle this yourself or hire someone to do it for you.

External Quality Assurance Visits

Following approval, you will receive your first EQA visit once you have learners who have been on the programme for a few months or who are nearing certification.

EQA visits will then occur at least annually, depending on the centre's risk rating and the type and number of qualifications being delivered. Arrangements will vary depending on the awarding organisation and their processes, but you are likely to receive a mixture of face-to-face and online visits.

External quality assurers (EQAs) work for awarding organisations to ensure that qualifications are correctly certificated and that candidates are assessed rigorously but fairly.

Before a visit, the EQA will be in touch, usually via the IQA or head of centre, to plan and organise what they will be doing during their visit. They will provide you with a visit agenda and a breakdown of what they need, such as access to facilities, staff and candidates for observation and feedback, the portfolios and learner work they want to see and what policies, procedures and meeting minutes they will require. They will also check your internal quality assurance processes to ensure your IQA(s) are carrying out their responsibilities correctly. Make sure you fully understand what your EQA wants during their visit so you can get things ready for them in advance.

One of the main checks during an EQA visit is the sampling of candidate portfolios, either online or paper-based. The EQA will look at the coursework submitted by candidates and compare it to the decisions made by your centre's assessors. This ensures that candidates receive the correct result, whether it is a competent pass for meeting standards or a referral for additional support. As part of this check, they will also need to see all the assessors' records and feedback, together with feedback the assessors have received from IQA observation and sampling.

The EQA will want to observe and speak with assessors to verify their skills and competence, ensuring they carry out their roles fairly and to the best of their abilities. They will be observed carrying out an observation of candidates and giving feedback with a clear statement of competence or non-competence to the candidate. The EQA will then observe the IQA, giving feedback and any developmental support to the assessor.

Often, candidates are also interviewed during the visit to discuss the course, assessments and progression. This helps to provide a comprehensive overview of the training centre's processes and procedures, as well as find out about the learners' journey. As with assessors, it is important to brief the candidates and make sure they understand that it is not them who are being checked but the centre and staff.

Once all of this has been completed, the EQA usually provides initial feedback directly to the head of centre, the IQA and sometimes the assessors. This is to brief them on what they have concluded, point out good practices that were found and advise on any improvements needed. They will sometimes give an initial indication of the risk rating they will be giving your centre.

Following your EQA visit, you will receive a detailed report compiled by the EQA. You normally receive this directly from the awarding organisation a few days after the visit has concluded.

This report will include details of all assessments carried out at your centre, including any action points required for the centre to improve and the overall rating assigned to your centre. Where applicable, it will also detail any qualifications you have achieved Direct Claim Status for. This means you will be able to claim certificates without waiting for an EQA visit or EQA approval each time. This document can serve as your guide to what is working well in your centre and what may need improvements.

The accreditation process also ensures compliance with standards through regular external quality assurance (EQA) visits and internal quality assurance practices. These measures ensure that your training programmes are consistently delivered to a high standard, benefiting both trainers and trainees. Furthermore, the emphasis on continuous professional development (CPD) ensures that your staff remains competent and up to date with industry developments.

Matrix Accreditation (Mandatory)

The matrix Standard, owned by the Department for Education (DfE), is all about making sure you're delivering top-notch information, advice, and guidance (IAG - Initial Advice and Guidance) services that help people reach their full potential. It's currently managed by the Growth Company and is relevant in any setting where initial advice and guidance are provided, including education.

Getting assessed against the matrix Standard gives you a nationally recognized stamp of approval for your IAG services. But it's more than just a badge—it's a chance to get valuable feedback on how to keep improving what you do. Achieving this standard shows that you're serious about quality, which not only helps attract more customers but is also often a must-have if you're going after government contracts or tenders.

In our own practice, we make sure to follow a thorough onboarding process that includes everything from a detailed brochure outlining what the learner will be getting into, to a comprehensive learner handbook that we'll dive into more in our policies chapter. We also provide an induction that can be done online or in person, where we cover everything—the qualification they'll be working towards, how they'll communicate with their tutors and assessors, and the entire process from start to finish, including on-programme and exit advice for their next steps.

The matrix Standard is built around seven key elements:

- Purpose
- Resource
- Offer
- Delivery
- Outcomes for individuals
- Impact for organisations
- Continuous Improvement

The initial cost for getting this accreditation is usually between £2,500 and £3,000, and it's valid for three years, with two annual reviews included. After that, re-accreditation every three years will cost you around £2,000, depending on the size of your organisation. It's important to factor these costs into your planning, especially since it's a mandatory requirement, whether you're working on a direct contract or as a subcontractor.

https://matrixstandard.com/standard/

Ofsted Grades

If you have a direct contract, you can expect to be inspected by Ofsted at least every five years—more frequently if your rating gets downgraded. That's why it's so important to be constantly preparing for these inspections and to include this in your strategic plans.

If you're a partner or subcontractor, there's a good chance you'll be questioned by the Ofsted team when they inspect the lead provider who you're contracting with. As a partner, Ofsted will consider you as part of the lead provider's team, so it's important to be prepared. I've always made a point of supporting our lead providers, since they're the ones awarding us contracts, and I truly believe that's been key to securing those contracts and maintaining strong relationships with them year after year.

Using the Ofsted framework to guide our quality procedures has been crucial for us. We regularly review other training providers' Ofsted reports to understand what works well and where we can improve. Inspections are likely to happen every few years, so it's important not to fear them. Instead, view Ofsted officers as outside auditors who are there to help you maintain and improve your standards.

I can't stress enough how valuable it is to work with an outside consultant to get you ready for an Ofsted inspection. Our consultant gave us a real head start, helping us understand what to expect and how to prepare. The investment paid off when we were awarded a Grade 2, marking us as a good provider. The sense of accomplishment and pride we felt was incredible, and I would highly recommend this approach.

A key part of our preparation was creating a clear, written Self-Assessment Report (SAR) each year. This was a joint effort with the team and laid the foundation for our Quality Improvement Plan (QIP). The QIP, with its clear goals and timeframes, is rolled out throughout the year, keeping us focused and continually improving. Achieving a good grade from Ofsted isn't just a validation of your hard work—it's a real buzz that makes you feel like you're on top of your game

In Conclusion

In conclusion, these accreditations and grades add significant value to your business, showing funders that you're a sustainable operation. Pursuing accredited qualifications has been a game-changer, unlocking funding opportunities and strengthening our market position. Beyond compliance, they've given us credibility, helping secure grants and loans. This investment has taught us a lot about long-term sustainability and has been well worth it.

Chapter 8

Creating a Dream Team for a Training Provider in England

I often hear from many businesses, even those generating over £1 million online, that they are hesitant to invest in a team and prefer to outsource most of their work. However, this approach often results in merely creating a profitable job, rather than a scalable business. Personally, since I invested in building my team, my turnover has **trebled,** and my profits have doubled. I passionately believe that investing in a skilled team will allow you to buy back time to work *on* your business instead of *in* it. For instance, hiring a £30,000 team member, if you choose them correctly, can easily add £100,000 to your bottom line.

When I had my first business, a nail salon, back in 2001, I grew this business to a team of seven using the principles I teach using apprenticeships and different funding pots. I went on to do the same in a total of five salons by upskilling hair stylists to be able to offer nail and beauty treatments, all using funded training.

For training providers delivering government-accredited and regulated training in England, building a high-performing team is absolutely crucial. Investing in the right people can seriously boost your business's ability to deliver quality training, improve client satisfaction, and drive growth—not to mention attract more funding. You might be wondering, what does this have to do with funding? Well, here's the deal: your retention rates, outcomes, achievements, and learner progression—whether they move on to higher qualifications or into work—are key factors that determine whether you'll win or keep future contracts.

We've learned this the hard way. We've had team members who jeopardised our outcomes and retention rates. I once had a rogue assessor who could talk the talk, but after she left a few weeks later, we quickly realised she couldn't teach. It was a tough lesson, but it reinforced the importance of having the right people in place.

Yes, building a solid team might seem costly at first, but believe me, the returns—in terms of efficiency, scalability, and profitability—make it all worth it. Plus, it sets you up with a business that will sell for a decent profit when you're ready to exit. It's all part of the journey, and from our experience, it's one of the best investments you can make in your business.

That's why I prefer to train my team. Repeatedly, I've seen that when we deliver the training—whether it's for a quality manager or a tutor—the quality is far higher. I take immense pride in building a system that develops people to be the best they can be by embedding our core values. We've built a team I'm extremely proud of, and this approach allows us to quickly identify those who can't be developed and let them go swiftly, thanks to the system we have put in place. Everything we do follows the same quality programs we teach, ensuring consistency and excellence.

The adage "there is no 'I' in 'team'" holds profound truth. Reflecting upon my journey, I realise how crucial it has been to build a team that is not only innovative but self-sufficient. I have nurtured a group that thinks independently and can be trusted to manage their tasks effectively without constant oversight.

To scale a business, being a good leader is far more critical than being a manager. A leader possesses a variety of qualities and skills that enable them to inspire and guide others towards achieving common goals. As a leader, you need to have a clear vision for the future and be able to communicate it effectively to others. Integrity is essential: being honest, ethical and leading by example. This is something often lacking in the political world, with significant negative impacts, and the same applies to business. If you don't adhere to your core values, you risk the business failing. I have experienced this firsthand and paid the price for not always sticking to my principles.

Good leaders also possess empathy, understanding and consideration for the feelings and perspectives of others. I have learned the importance of making decisions promptly and confidently. Once committed, you must see them through. A lot of time can be lost in dithering, and while some decisions will lead to success and others to failure, each will teach you something valuable. Clear communication is vital: you need to convey your ideas effectively and listen actively to your team's challenges and ideas, helping them find solutions.

One of the most rewarding aspects of leadership for me has been motivating and inspiring others to achieve their best. Watching my competition grow and become their best has been one of my greatest joys. Being adaptable and open to change is crucial, especially when working with government-funded training, where things change frequently. You must pivot quickly so your team feels secure, knowing you will steer the ship to calmer waters when needed.

Accountability is another critical trait. Great leaders take responsibility for their actions and decisions and trust their team, delegating tasks effectively. When mistakes happen, it's essential to keep your emotions in check. Early on, I found this challenging because mistakes often cost money, and coming from a place of scarcity made this more challenging. However, if you are good at what you do, plenty of money can be made. Allow your team to learn from their mistakes, implement systems to prevent them from happening again and move on. This approach develops a culture where team members feel confident making decisions without constantly seeking approval.

In summary, leadership is about having a clear vision, integrity, empathy, decisiveness, clear communication, the ability to inspire, adaptability, accountability and trust. These qualities have shaped my journey, allowing me to grow and scale my business effectively.

Once I realised that management was not for me and began delegating to managers, the business flourished. A good manager implements the leader's vision through effective planning, organising and coordinating resources. While leaders focus on inspiring and guiding the team, managers maintain stability and optimise existing processes. They oversee operations and ensure tasks are completed efficiently, often being more risk-averse and concentrating on minimising risks and ensuring smooth operations. By working within established frameworks to solve problems, managers play a crucial role in maintaining the steady progress and efficiency of the business. Reflecting upon my journey, it became clear that empowering capable managers was key to our success.

In my opinion, for a business to be successful, you need both strong leadership and effective management. You need several skilled senior managers, a business strategist, a visionary and a mobiliser. When Julie joined my business, she brought management skills to the table. Initially, Julie worked part-time as a trainer, managing her apprentices. After reading her CV and realising her vast management experience, I knew she was the perfect candidate to run the training team. At first, she refused the job, but I can be very persuasive. She eventually agreed to work part-time for a couple of days a week. Within six months, she became full-time, sold her business and bought into mine. This was in 2011, and I thank my lucky stars every day I met her. We are like Yin and Yang, and I honestly believe that is what makes it work.

When I look at my management team, I realise I have always had a relationship with them first, understanding their values before they started working for me. Lewis, for example, was the grandson of my long-time employee Jayne. He trained as an apprentice in another business but was trained by us and, reflecting upon Jayne's values as an employee and knowing him personally, I knew I could develop him. He was easily coached.

Rhys, my son, is training to become my sales manager. After working for many years with a hair and beauty wholesaler as a rep, he shares many of the same attributes in sales. He is well-liked, personable, very honest and persuasive, easily closing sales. He also has the organisational skills needed as a manager, something I have always struggled with. Although I have learned these skills, they did not come easily to me. I still recognise that if it's something I don't enjoy doing, I can easily get distracted, so now I delegate those tasks.

Finally, Danni is our quality training manager. Her passion for great training and her love for her team shows that if you employ the right people, their passion, drive and belief in the business will help your business grow quicker. For me, training from within has always worked. I am not saying you cannot find managers through recruiting; I can only reflect on my experience. Once you know someone, it's easier to know if they are right for your business.

Therefore, I choose to delegate managerial tasks to skilled managers. This delegation allows me to concentrate on my core strengths: strategic planning, innovation and driving the business's vision. By leaving my skilled managers to handle day-to-day operations, I ensure that the business runs smoothly and efficiently.

What is the Secret to Creating an Effective Team?

This involves making many mistakes and learning from them. In my experience, building a successful team requires perseverance and resilience. Even after twenty-five years in business, I still don't have all the answers, and I frequently encounter challenges. This is not a cause for despondency; it is a crucial part of the journey. What I've gained from these experiences are valuable lessons, which I now share with my management team.

The first key to building a dedicated team is ensuring everyone understands your company's vision and goals. This sense of purpose provides clear direction. Each year, I outline our vision and goals for the coming year and the next three years to keep everyone aligned. We hold quarterly Senior Management Team (SMT) meetings to break down our objectives into specific responsibilities, including strategy, marketing, sales, operations, compliance and quality, and financials. Each SMT member is accountable for one area. While it might not initially be feasible to have senior managers for every role, the aim is to generate sufficient revenue—around £45k to £50k per role by 2025—to support this structure.

In the early days, I lacked a clear vision, had not considered my exit strategy and often blamed external factors for setbacks. Over time, my approach evolved. Initially, I micromanaged and worked excessively long hours, relying heavily on word-of-mouth for growth. My desire for success was strong, but I never formalised it. The COVID lockdown, when I was fifty-six, was a turning point. I realised that if I didn't change, my business would have no future without me. I began investing in my team, starting with my personal development. This shift allowed me to delegate effectively and focus on scaling the business.

Raising capital was crucial for these investments, and we recently secured an additional £100K through the Growth Fund to help us further develop our business. Since we're creating employment, this funding comes as an interest-free loan, a fantastic boost. On top of that, because we've been focusing on developing digital skills within the business, we partnered with another organisation to create a Multi-Platform Apprenticeship program.

One of my mentors, Danny Wicks, really drove home the importance of recruiting the right people and placing them in roles that align with their strengths and passions. I shifted from making decisions based on instinct to focusing on return on investment. Now, I'm building a business that can thrive without me, with the goal of eventually selling or stepping back entirely. This approach ensures a recurring income, giving me the freedom to pursue my interests while the business continues to grow.

When Julie, the other director, and I started building the team, we began by mapping out all the senior roles in the training business and detailing their responsibilities. The two of us had been juggling all these roles, which led us to create an organisational structure in 2020. Our first step was figuring out which roles generated the most revenue. For me, that was innovation, sales, and marketing; for Julie, it was managing finances, profit and loss, and cash flow. We knew we needed to replace ourselves in the other roles as quickly as possible.

Our first hire focused on quality operations and compliance, and then we expanded the sales team. We figured if we could boost sales, we'd eventually generate enough income to replace ourselves in the other roles, like marketing and HR.

While we haven't fully replaced ourselves in all roles yet, we've made significant progress. I'm still overseeing marketing and sales, but I'm grooming a Sales Manager and a Marketing Manager to handle data monitoring and collection—and guess what? They're all doing apprenticeships from Level 5 to Level 6. As our sales team has grown over the past three years, Julie has successfully handed off her responsibilities in compliance and most of the quality and operations tasks. She's now focused on supporting our Senior Management Team and developing them with Level 5 Leadership apprenticeships, which will only improve their management skills further. And the best part? We're getting paid by the government to do this.

This transition has taken time, and investment, but now we have got a clear, documented plan with financial goals and timelines for fully delegating these roles. We are well on our way, and it's exciting to see the progress.

Building the Foundation & The different roles

In any educational institution, the foundation is built upon a dedicated team, with each member bringing unique skills and expertise to the table. When I started this journey, my initial focus was on sales and marketing. However, as we grew, the importance of having a structured and well-rounded team became evident. I will reflect below on the various roles that have become essential in our organisation and how we have developed these positions to ensure excellence and innovation in our educational offerings.

It is important to note that this will not be achieved overnight. By drawing out an organisational plan for what you want your business to look like in three, five and ten years, you will reach your goals more efficiently. Remember: if you fail to plan, you plan to fail.

Head of Training

Our head of training is responsible for enhancing curriculum development, maintaining academic standards and encouraging innovation and excellence in our educational programmes. This role involves identifying team members' potential, training them and developing them into excellent trainers. In our experience, we have broken this down by vocational roles to ensure specialised attention. For example, in the hair and beauty training business, we have a head of hair and a head of beauty. This approach has allowed us to tailor training and development to each area, ensuring that each department thrives under dedicated leadership.

Trainers and Instructors

From the outset, I decided that our trainers and instructors must remain active in their vocational fields. This ensures they bring current industry knowledge and skills to their teaching. Our trainers deliver high-quality training sessions, create course materials and assess learners. Their primary goal is to ensure student success and engagement, creating a supportive and effective learning environment. I am passionate about using government funding to build a strong team, particularly through our Teaching and Learning Skills Apprenticeship programme. This initiative has proven invaluable for training our trainers. For instance, Rayner, one of my trainers, started her journey with us in this way. Similarly, Rebecca, one of her peers, showed remarkable enthusiasm and dedication, always completing her coursework on time and with great attention to detail. Their commitment really highlights how effective our approach is. We also use the Mentoring apprenticeship to further develop their communication skills, and through these qualifications, we've seen significant progress in the retention and achievements of their learners—something that directly helps us secure larger funding pots.

Student Support and Admissions Coordinator

Currently, Anne is our Student Support and Admissions Coordinator, providing guidance and support to all our students throughout their learning journey. She ensures their needs are met with a student-centric approach, and she manages the enrolment process, making sure new students are onboarded smoothly. Anne is a great example of collaboration and efficiency in everything she does. We're now developing her further so she can eventually lead future coordinators, and to enhance her client skills, she's taking the Level 3 Customer Service apprenticeship.

Marketing and Outreach

We have now found a potential marketing manager, Kadi, who already has some skills in management and marketing. For a long time, I handled this role with the help of marketing friends. Kadi will develop and implement strategies to attract new students, emphasising integrity and transparency in all promotional activities. Our plan is to develop their team using the Multi-Platform Apprenticeship and Content Creation Apprenticeship, ensuring we stay ahead in our marketing efforts.

Sales Team

Our sales team has seen the most significant growth this year. We employed a lead generator and two new sales associates, and I am currently developing one of them to take over the sales management role. Although I still oversee this aspect, as it is my favourite part of the role, I have outsourced some responsibilities. However, my plan now is to expand this part of the business, there being such a call for salespeople, and for the Level 4 Sales Executive Apprenticeship, so my sales manager will complete the B2B Sales Executive Apprenticeship, which will benefit most businesses.

Administrative and Technical Support

Jayne, our long-term Administrative Assistant, has been with me for over twenty years. She provides administrative support to all our staff and students, ensuring efficiency and reliability in daily operations. We are currently employing an apprentice to join our team and develop them through the Level 3 Customer Service Apprenticeship, ensuring continued quality in our administrative support.

For information technology (IT) support, we rely on Signet for our training, our training systems, a system called PICS and Go High Level for our marketing and sales automation. These specialists maintain our technical infrastructure and support our online learning platforms, embracing innovation to enhance the learning experience.

Building and Nurturing Your Team

Recruitment Strategies

One of the key factors in our success so far has been embedding our core values into our team, starting with the recruitment of an exceptional training team. Our main values—Passion for Learning, Keeping it Real, Committing to Success and Going Above and Beyond—are integral to all our job descriptions. We not only recruit based on skills but look for these values in all our interview questions.

Our recruitment process begins with advertising the position and having our operations team sift through applications, looking for evidence of candidates who embody our values. This is followed by an initial telephone call to further assess suitability. Once we have a shortlist, we conduct group interviews with several members of the management team. For Senior Management Team (SMT) positions, Julie and I conduct the interviews ourselves, seeking strong managers who complement our strengths while upholding our core values.

In the past, I made the mistake of hiring people based on personal liking rather than core skills and attitude, which often resulted in costly mistakes. Now, during group interviews, we set several tasks and observe how candidates interact with each other.

It is crucial that our team demonstrates the following skills:

1. **Integrity**: Committing to ethical practices and compliance with regulations.
2. **Excellence**: Striving for the highest standards in training, delivery and support.
3. **Collaboration**: Fostering a team-oriented environment to enhance learning outcomes.
4. **Innovation**: Embracing new methods and technologies to improve training effectiveness.
5. **Student-Centric Approach**: Prioritising the needs and success of students.

By focusing on these qualities, we ensure that our team is not only skilled but aligned with our core values, setting the foundation for continued success.

Recruiting the right people is crucial for the success and growth of any organisation. Over the years, I have refined our recruitment process, ensuring we select individuals who not only possess the necessary skills but align with our values and culture.

The Competency Interview and Project

The final part of our recruitment process is the competency interview and project. Unlike traditional interviews that rely on standard questions, we focus on competency-based questions. These questions require candidates to reflect upon their past experiences, providing real examples of how they have successfully navigated challenges or achieved goals. This method helps us ascertain their honesty and ability to think critically about their experiences.

The Role of Neuro-Linguistic Programming (NLP)

My journey in improving our recruitment process led me to study neuro-linguistic programming (NLP). This knowledge has been invaluable during interviews, allowing me to quickly discern if a candidate is genuinely recalling an experience or fabricating a story. In the past, my trusting nature often led me to believe candidates who told me what I wanted to hear. However, by incorporating NLP techniques, I can better gauge the authenticity of their responses, ensuring we select candidates who are honest and capable.

Developing Competency Questions

Crafting competency questions that make candidates think deeply about their past actions has been a game-changer. These questions prompt them to provide specific examples of times when they faced problems or challenges and how they overcame them. This approach reveals not only their problem-solving skills but also their ability to articulate and reflect upon their experiences.

DISC Personality Assessment

In addition to competency questions, we utilise the DISC personality assessment. This tool helps us understand the different personality types and the skills they are likely to possess. The DISC model categorises individuals into four types: Red, Yellow, Green and Blue, each representing different traits and strengths.

The book *Surrounded by Idiots* has been instrumental in our understanding of these personality types. By studying and applying the DISC assessment, we ensure that each job role attracts candidates with the right skills and personality traits. This alignment has significantly improved our recruitment outcomes, ensuring we have the right people in the right roles.

Refining our recruitment process has been a journey of continuous learning and adaptation. By incorporating competency-based questions, NLP techniques and the DISC personality assessment, we have developed a robust system that helps us select the right candidates. These tools and techniques have improved our hiring outcomes and enhanced our team's overall effectiveness.

As we continue to grow, we remain committed to using these strategies to build a strong, capable and cohesive workforce.

Team Development Plan

At our company, we are committed to the continuous development and excellence of our team. Here is our structured approach to nurturing talent across various departments through funded courses and apprenticeships:

Marketing Team

- **Initial Training:** All members start with the **Level 3 Multi-Platform Marketing Apprenticeship** and **Content Creation Apprenticeship**.
- **Progression Path:** After completing the initial training, they advance to the **Marketing Manager** level.

Sales Team

- **Initial Training:** The team begins with the **Level 4 Sales Executive Apprenticeship**.
- **Progression Path:** Upon completion, they progress to the **Level 6 B2B Sales Professional**.

Training Team

- **Initial Training:** Team members are trained with the **Level 3 Teachers Award in Education**.
- **Progression Path:**
    a. They move on to the **Level 3 Learning Skills Apprenticeship**.

   b. Afterward, they proceed to the **Level 4 Mentoring**.
   c. Finally, they specialise in one of the following:
      - **Level 5 Teaching**
      - **Level 5 Coaching**
      - **Internal Quality Assurer (IQA)** qualifications

- **Continuous Skills Training:** In addition to the above, all training team members will attend various forms of skills training tailored to their specific vocational expertise. This ensures our training team holds all the relevant and trending skills to keep our training programmes up to date with the latest industry standards.

Admin and Customer Service Team

- **Initial Training:** They begin with the **Level 2 Customer Service Practitioner Apprenticeship**.
- **Progression Path:** They then advance to the **Level 3 Customer Service Specialist**.

Management Team

- **Training Path:** All management team members develop through the **Operations and Departmental Manager Standard**.

Continuous Training and Development

- **Ongoing Training:** We invest in continuous training and development to ensure our staff remain at the forefront of industry standards and innovations.
- **Encouraging Excellence:** We provide opportunities for staff to enhance their skills and knowledge, promoting a culture of continuous improvement and excellence.

Core Value: Passion for Learning

Once we employ someone, we don't stop there. We have access to extensive funded training, and one of our core values is a Passion for Learning. This ensures that our team members continually grow and excel in their roles, promoting a lifelong commitment to learning and development.

Positive Impact

We have encouraged people to join our team by implementing this comprehensive development plan. We know they have been developed to the highest standard, even if they move on to new opportunities. Many of our former employees have returned to us for further training or have recommended us to others, reflecting the lasting impact of our commitment to their growth.

Successful Training Providers: Building High-Performing Teams

To illustrate the effectiveness of our development plan, let us look at some successful training providers in England that have built high-performing teams. Here are a few examples and the lessons we can learn from their core values and commitment to team excellence:

1. Kaplan

Overview: Kaplan is a leading provider of professional qualifications and apprenticeships in the UK. They offer a wide range of training programmes, including accountancy, finance and business apprenticeships.

Core Values and Team Excellence:

- **Continuous Learning:** Kaplan fosters a culture of lifelong learning among its employees. They provide extensive training and professional development opportunities to ensure staff stay current with industry standards.
- **Innovation:** Kaplan encourages innovation by adopting new technologies and teaching methods, which enhances both teaching effectiveness and learner engagement.
- **Supportive Environment:** Kaplan prioritises creating a supportive work environment where staff feel valued and motivated to achieve their best.

Key Takeaways:

- Invest in continuous learning and professional development.
- Embrace innovation and new technologies.
- Create a supportive and motivating work environment.

2. The Skills Network

Overview: The Skills Network is a renowned provider of online learning and skills training in the UK. They offer a wide array of courses in various sectors, including health and social care, business and education.

Core Values and Team Excellence:

- **Flexibility:** The Skills Network promotes flexible working conditions, which helps in attracting and retaining top talent.
- **Quality Assurance:** They maintain high standards of quality assurance, ensuring all training programmes are up to date and meet industry requirements.
- **Employee Development:** The company emphasises the importance of employee development through regular training sessions and opportunities for career advancement.

Key Takeaways:

- Promote flexible working conditions.
- Maintain high standards of quality assurance.
- Emphasise continuous employee development.

Lessons Learned: Key Takeaways

Core Values:

- **Passion for Learning:** Continuous learning and professional development are crucial for building high-performing teams.
- **Innovation:** Embracing new technologies and innovative practices enhances teaching effectiveness and learner engagement.
- **Supportive Environment:** Creating a supportive and flexible work environment helps attract and retain top talent.
- **Quality Assurance:** Maintaining high standards of quality assurance ensures training programmes are relevant and effective.
- **Customer Focus:** Understanding and meeting the needs of the client drives excellence in service delivery.
- **Employee Empowerment:** Empowering employees through growth opportunities and a culture of feedback fosters a motivated and high-performing team.
- **Collaboration:** Encouraging collaboration and knowledge sharing leads to a stronger, more cohesive team.

By learning from these successful funded training providers, we can continue to refine our development plan, ensuring our team remains at the forefront of industry standards and continues to deliver excellence in all areas.

Challenges and Solutions

Building and managing a high-performing team in the training industry comes with its own set of challenges. Here are some common issues that we have often faced, along with strategies that we have used to address them:

Attracting Qualified Talent

Challenges:

- **Skill Shortages:** Finding candidates with the right mix of qualifications and experience can be difficult.
- **Competition:** Competing with other organisations for top talent can be challenging, especially in specialised fields.

Strategies:

- We have overcome the challenge of attracting and retaining skilled professionals by offering competitive salaries and benefits, as well as performance-based commissions. For example, commissions are based on learner retention and completion for trainers, and on marketing and sales achievements for sales and marketing staff. In customer service, we use a net promoter score system, contacting clients quarterly via phone or email surveys to rate us from one to five. This feedback helps us reward our team appropriately.

- During our advertising and recruitment process, we highlight opportunities for growth within the organisation. Monthly one-to-one meetings and yearly appraisals, where we measure KPIs relevant to each job role and company value, also emphasise development opportunities. This approach not only attracts ambitious candidates but helps retain them.
- Additionally, we offer flexible working arrangements to appeal to a broader range of candidates, including opportunities to work from home and set schedules that suit their needs. This flexibility has proven essential in building a dedicated and satisfied team.

Retaining Skilled Employees

Challenges:

- **High Turnover Rates:** The training industry can experience high turnover, which disrupts continuity and quality.
- **Burnout:** Trainers and educators can face burnout due to high workloads and stress.

Strategies:

We hold quarterly recognition programmes to reward and acknowledge our team's contributions with vouchers and holidays. Each year, individuals who achieve exceptional results are rewarded through a bonus system for high achievers.

We promote a healthy work-life balance through flexible scheduling and workload management. Additionally, we frequently hold wellbeing events, both online and in person, and provide access to a counselling service for those going through difficult times.

Every role in our organisation comes with clear career pathways and opportunities for advancement, ensuring that our team members can see a future with us and feel motivated to grow within the company.

Keeping Skills and Knowledge Up to Date

Challenges:

- **Rapid Industry Changes:** Keeping up with the latest industry trends, technologies and best practices is crucial, but challenging.
- **Continuous Professional Development:** Ensuring that all team members regularly update their skills can be difficult to manage.

Strategies:

One of the advantages of being a training provider is that we invest heavily in regular training programmes and ongoing professional development for our staff. One of our core values is a Passion for Learning, which helps us attract individuals who share this enthusiasm. While some may leave, the majority stay and grow with us.

We partner with industry bodies and professional organisations to stay abreast of the latest developments. This ensures that our training remains current and relevant, continuously developing our team with the new skills needed for their roles.

Additionally, we encourage a culture of knowledge sharing and continuous learning within the team. Many of our trainers become mentors to others, providing peer feedback and creating an environment where everyone is committed to personal and professional growth. This dedication to learning and mentorship is a cornerstone of our core values.

High-Quality and Consistent Training for Your Team

<u>Challenges:</u>

- **Quality Assurance:** Maintaining high standards of training across all programmes and trainers can be challenging.
- **Standardisation:** Ensuring consistency in training delivery and content across different trainers and locations.

<u>Strategies:</u>

Being an accredited and regulated training provider has ensured we have robust quality assurance processes. We regularly invite external stakeholders into the business to provide feedback for continuous improvement. An Ofsted officer recently advised me to view inspections as free consultancy opportunities to further enhance our practices. This mindset has helped us implement comprehensive quality assurance processes to monitor and maintain high standards.

We have standardised training materials and a curriculum that can be rolled out to our new partners as we open satellite centres across England. These partners gain access to all our systems, allowing them to grow much faster with our support and help.

We also conduct regular audits and gather feedback from learners, employers, staff and partners. This continuous feedback loop enables us to improve not only our training but the systems and processes we share, ensuring excellence throughout our organisation.

Managing Remote and Hybrid Teams

Challenges:

- **Communication:** Ensuring effective communication and collaboration among team members who may be working remotely or in various locations.
- **Engagement:** Keeping remote employees engaged and motivated can be difficult.

Strategies:

The landscape of business in the last five years has changed, and that is why any growing business must start to utilise digital collaboration tools to facilitate communication and teamwork.

The 2020 lockdowns due to COVID-19 taught us valuable lessons about remote work. When most of our training team worked from home to deliver training, we found that regular scheduled check-ins and virtual meetings helped maintain a sense of connection and engagement among team members. This experience has proven invaluable as we now work with employees in India and various locations across England, significantly improving our scalability and operational efficiency.

Providing training on best practices in remote work ensures that everyone is equipped to work efficiently and effectively from any location. By embracing these strategies, our training business—and yours—can adapt to the evolving landscape and continue to thrive.

Adapting to Technological Advancements

Challenges:

- **Integration:** Integrating new technologies into existing training programmes can be complex and resource-intensive.
- **Training on New Technologies:** Ensuring that trainers are proficient in new technologies and can teach them effectively.

Strategies:

With so many modern technologies constantly evolving, it's essential to gradually integrate them into training programmes to allow time for adjustment. Providing comprehensive training for the team on innovative technologies and tools is crucial. By establishing feedback loops during one-to-one training sessions and regular weekly team meetings, we can assess the effectiveness of these recent technologies and make necessary adjustments. This approach ensures a smooth transition and continuous improvement in our training processes.

Balancing Cost and Quality

Challenges:

- **Budget Constraints:** Balancing the need for high-quality training with budgetary limitations can be challenging.
- **Resource Allocation:** Efficiently allocating resources to various training programmes and initiatives.

Strategies:

Quality is crucial, but profitability is equally important. Therefore, all our courses are closely monitored by our finance and operations team, who identify and implement cost-effective training solutions, such as online learning platforms, to improve our bottom line. By understanding which courses generate the largest profits, we can prioritise investment in training areas that will have the most significant impact on quality and outcomes.

Additionally, it is important to monitor all our financial KPIs. Through thorough financial planning and budgeting, we can ensure sustainable investment in training, balancing quality with profitability to support the long-term success of our organisation.

By understanding and addressing these common challenges, you, as a training provider, can build and manage high-performing teams that deliver exceptional training and development programmes, allowing you to scale your business effectively.

Conclusion

In this chapter, we talked about how crucial it is to build a high-performing team if you want to run a successful funded training provider business. I can't stress enough how important it is to invest in the right people—it really pays off in terms of efficiency, scalability, and profitability.

Here is a summary:

- Delegate management tasks to skilled managers so everything runs smoothly.
- Offer competitive salaries, benefits, and performance-based commissions to attract and retain top talent.
- Provide clear career pathways and plenty of opportunities for professional development.
- Promote a healthy work-life balance by offering flexible working arrangements.
- Implement strong quality assurance processes and always seek feedback to keep improving.

- Use digital collaboration tools and best practices for remote work, and gradually bring in new technologies with proper training and feedback.
- Keep an eye on financial KPIs and focus your investments on the most profitable training areas to ensure sustainable growth.

I can tell you from experience that achieving excellence in training and development programs comes with a few bumps along the way. I've learned a lot from my mistakes, but I've also learned that success hinges on strong core values and teamwork. By promoting a culture of continuous learning, sharing knowledge, and working together, you can build a resilient, high-performing team. The added bonus? With the value of apprenticeships ranging between £5,000 and £15,000, you're actually getting paid to train your own staff using government funding. When everyone is driven by a passion for learning and a commitment to quality, that collective effort will push your business forward and ensure long-term success.

Chapter 9

Marketing and Sales Strategy for funded training providers

Why This Chapter Matters

The reason I included this chapter in a book about funding is that, without a clear marketing and sales strategy, no amount of funding will lead to growth in enrolments and sales. For me, sales are the most critical part of the journey, which is why I have a dedicated team focused on generating sales. They are rewarded accordingly because they produce revenue.

In this chapter, I share our sales journey and provide practical insights and real-life examples to offer a blueprint for growing your enrolments. By sharing our experiences, successes and lessons learned, I aim to guide and inspire you on your path to effective marketing and business growth.

A few years ago, I read the book *Blue Ocean Strategy*, and it made me realise that the way I had created my marketing & sales strategy for my training business was exactly what the authors described. Since then, I've been teaching my mentees this strategy, showing them how to carve out unique and niche market spaces for sustainable growth and success.

So what is the blue ocean strategy? It is a business approach that encourages businesses to create new market spaces, or 'blue oceans', where there's no competition, instead of fighting in overcrowded markets, or 'red oceans'. It is all about innovation and offering something unique that makes the competition irrelevant.

What Are the Key Principles of the Strategy?

So, how can you duplicate it? It is about creating a giant leap in value for clients, making competitors irrelevant. You do this by finding new demand in unexplored market spaces instead of competing in crowded markets. Focus on the overall vision and innovative ideas, not just the numbers. Understand why non-clients are not buying and tap into their unmet needs. Finally, make sure your offering's utility, price, cost and adoption are all spot on to build a viable new product or service. This approach helped me grow my business, and it can do the same for you.

Example Application:

When I launched a new product aimed at salon owners using government funding for training programmes, I didn't compete with other training providers. Instead, I targeted a specific niche: established salon operators wanting to offer in-house training. This created a blue ocean by addressing a unique need, avoiding direct competition and creating new demand.

By focusing on creating value in an uncontested space, the blue ocean strategy helps businesses find new growth opportunities and achieve sustainable success.

But what does this mean for small business owners? How can entrepreneurs apply these principles to set themselves apart and achieve unprecedented growth?

Let me share my journey and how I adapted my strategy over the last four years. I specialise in training individuals with a particular expertise in various fields to become teachers, assessors and mentors. After training them, I pay them to deliver our training programmes in satellite locations. Here is how it works:

1. **Training and Certification**: I train professionals on what they need to become certified, funded training providers.
2. **Partnership and Support**: These professionals come under the TNB Skills umbrella. For a monthly charge, they gain access to all our procedures, policies and the full support of my team.
3. **Mutual Benefits**: This partnership is mutually beneficial. The trainers get to do what they

love—delivering quality training—and are paid significantly for their services. They also have the opportunity to become full subcontractors or pursue their own contracts.

4. **Expanded Reach**: We gain specialised trainers who can deliver quality training across the country. Additionally, we can rent their facilities, expanding our reach and capacity.
5. **Access to Funding**: Trainers gain access to funding, allowing them to deliver training to their clients nationwide.

This strategy has been a win-win for both parties. We get the benefit of their expertise and facilities, and they get the resources and support they need to succeed.

By niching down and creating a blue ocean strategy, we have become known as the experts in our field.

I have done this several times by specialising and using my expertise. During the COVID-19 pandemic, I supported salon owners facing unprecedented challenges. I grew a Facebook group of over seven hundred salons by sharing business insights and vital information about grants, bounce-back loans and pricing strategies for additional PPE costs upon reopening.

When the government announced a £2,000 grant for businesses taking on apprentices, I reached out to these salon owners, who had lost staff during the pandemic; many employees had become self-employed or found new jobs and didn't return. By providing crucial information and guidance on apprenticeships, I became known as the 'Apprenticeship Godmother' and a funding expert. I realised many businesses didn't know how to incorporate funding into their training models. This led me to develop my new foundation, signature and elite packages, helping businesses create their own training programmes and become training providers.

My expertise extended beyond social media: even four years later, salon owners frequently tag me for help with funding. My knowledge also led to writing opportunities for Salon Education, where I shared insights about apprenticeships.

My story shows the power of niche expertise in building a strong, loyal community. By focusing on the specific needs of salon owners and providing valuable resources, I established myself as a trusted authority in the industry. This specialisation not only helped my business grow but supported others in navigating the challenges of the pandemic and beyond.

This journey highlights the importance of understanding and meeting your target audience's specific needs. By doing so, niche businesses can carve out their own spaces in crowded markets, build loyal customer bases and achieve sustainable growth.

Understanding Your Target Audience

Reflecting upon my marketing and sales strategies, I recognise some initial mistakes when I first ventured into business, which I hope to help you avoid by sharing my story. Having previously worked as an area sales manager for Avon Cosmetics, my main task involved recruiting fifteen representatives every ten days, with a personal goal to exceed that number. Avon provided me with a customer list, and my duty was to visit each household door to door. However, I quickly realised the inefficiencies of this method, as most people were not home during my visits. This led me to adapt my strategy by targeting a specific demographic: mothers in their thirties who had just dropped their children at school. These encounters at school gates were far more productive and allowed me to network effectively through referrals.

This early career experience taught me the importance of identifying and focusing on an ideal client.

Understanding the specific needs and pain points of clients is crucial. This led to the creation of targeted lead magnets and sales funnels using digital marketing tools like Click Funnels, Active Campaign and Go High Level. These tools were key in scaling our operations. However, I learned that the success of paid advertising, such as Pay-Per-Click campaigns, relied heavily on the organic traction of the ads. This insight shifted our strategy to focus on organic growth before heavily investing in paid channels.

Collaborations with experts like Lisa Johnson, who specialises in maximising client acquisition through refined marketing strategies, were also vital. Her courses helped streamline our approach and maximise our return on investment. This emphasised the importance of aligning with professionals whose values and methods match our business philosophy.

Overall, my journey in marketing and sales has been one of continuous learning and adaptation. It highlighted the need to strategically focus on well-defined client profiles and engage them with solutions that address their unique challenges and aspirations.

Why Have a Sales and Marketing Strategy for a Funded Training Academy?

Developing a sales and marketing strategy for a funded training academy is crucial for several key reasons. Firstly, it enables us to accurately plan the number of students required to meet our targets and identify additional funding opportunities that may need to be explored. One of the fundamental principles of managing government funding is ensuring it is spent within the allocated timeframes. Failure to do so risks the unspent funds being reallocated to another provider, potentially resulting in reduced funding in the following year. Therefore, a well-defined strategy is essential, allowing us to develop a contingency plan should our initial efforts fall short.

For instance, consider a funding stream targeting short, four-day taster courses designed for 25-32-year-old women who have recently had children and are hesitant to return to full-time employment. These women may be seeking flexible job opportunities that fit around their family commitments but are uncertain whether the hair and beauty sector is the right fit for them.

To support this model, it was necessary to find a compatible funding stream. We achieved this by utilising a government initiative focused on quick employability programmes. This led us to identify Multiply funding, a priority within the gov.uk UK Shared Prosperity Fund, which aims to improve individuals' numeracy skills. The expectation tied to this funding is that it will be used to enhance functional numeracy levels in a measurable way. We created a programme in which a full day would be spent showing women between the ages of twenty-five and thirty-five transferable skills, such as how to price services and use profit and loss templates to ensure they are profitable. We then would add basic hair or beauty skills for a further two days so they could get a taste without making a long-term commitment. This also helped them build relationships and trust with the academy, which was part of our marketing and sales strategy. The end goal of this programme was to progress on to our fully-funded, twenty-eight-week adult education programme on hair or nail courses and then, once finished, progress further to our L3 & L4 advanced loans and then into salons or start their own business. We also gave funding for this—it increases the life-time value of each client, enabling us to warrant up-front marketing and sales costs.

By offering these taster courses, we can attract potential students who fit this demographic.

A well-thought-out sales and marketing strategy ensures we can effectively reach our target audience, plan for necessary resources and adjust our approach to achieve our goals.

This was our plan:

Week 1: Research and Planning

- **Identify Target Audience**: Focus on 25-32-year-old women who have recently had children and are seeking flexible job opportunities.
- **Set Goals**: Aim to recruit 70% of taster course participants into the twenty-eight-week hair or beauty adult education course.
- **Develop Content**: Create engaging content highlighting the benefits of a career in hair and beauty, success stories and details about the taster course.

Week 2: Digital Marketing Launch

- **Social Media Ads**: Launch targeted ads on Facebook and Instagram, focusing on local communities and parenting groups.
- **Email Marketing**: Send out emails to existing mailing lists and partner organisations, highlighting the new taster courses.
- **Website Update**: Ensure the academy's website has detailed information about the taster courses, an easy registration process and testimonials from past students.

Week 3: Community Engagement

- **Webinars and Live Q&A Sessions**: Host live sessions on Facebook and Instagram where interested participants can ask questions about the taster courses and the benefits of a career in hair and beauty.

- **Local Outreach**: Partner with local childcare centres, mothers' groups and community centres to distribute flyers and promote the taster courses.

Week 4: Content Marketing

- **Blog Posts and Articles**: Publish blog posts on the academy's website and guest posts on parenting and local community blogs about the benefits of flexible careers in hair and beauty.
- **Success Stories**: Share stories on social media and the websites of women who transitioned into a career in hair and beauty after attending the academy.

Week 5: Registration Push

- **Reminder Emails**: Send reminder emails to those who have shown interest but haven't registered yet.
- **Social Media Countdown**: Create a countdown on social media to build urgency and encourage last-minute sign-ups.
- **Incentives**: Offer a limited-time extra such as a free gel colour day or early-bird special for those who sign up within the week.

Week 6: Final Engagement and Follow-Up

- **Final Webinars**: Host a final online seminar to answer any last-minute questions and provide additional information about the taster courses.

- **Follow-Up Calls**: Reach out to interested participants via phone to offer personalised assistance with registration.
- **Thank You and Next Steps**: Send thank-you emails to all participants, outlining the next steps and what they can expect from the taster course.

Post-Campaign: Evaluation and Transition

- **Evaluate Campaign Success**: Analyse data on registrations, engagement and conversions to assess the campaign's success.
- **Feedback Collection**: Collect feedback from participants on their experience and how the campaign could be improved.
- **Transition to Full Courses**: Begin the process of transitioning taster course participants into the full twenty-eight-week hair or beauty adult education course, providing them with all necessary information and support.

By following this six-week campaign, we can effectively reach our target audience, engage them with valuable content and convert them into long-term students, ensuring the success of our funded training academy.

The Importance of Outreach Sales

One of my key strategies for business growth is outreach. Outreach sales are a proactive and strategic approach to acquiring new clients or customers. Although many businesses ignore this method, it has always been a focus for me. This approach allowed me to grow my business to £400,000 without any social media presence at all. In fact, until March 2020, I had no business social media presence. Many small businesses rely solely on inbound leads, waiting for potential clients to come to them. However, outreach sales involve actively engaging with individuals or businesses that fit your target audience or customer profile.

Proactive outreach can take various forms, including cold calls, email campaigns, direct messaging on social media, networking events and personalised communication. The goal is to initiate meaningful conversations, build relationships and convert prospects into loyal clients. This strategy is essential for businesses seeking to expand their customer base.

Developing the 16-18 Study Programme

Engaging with salon owners through outreach led me to introduce a new income stream called the traineeship study programme. When I first started, I realised that many young apprentices lacked the communication and confidence skills needed for success. To address this, I developed a 16-18 study programme for 16-18-year-olds not in education or training. This programme teaches employability skills and provides work experience, allowing us to build strong relationships with salon owners. These young people improve their communication and confidence, and many progress to full apprenticeship programmes upon completion.

The Benefits of Outreach Sales

Outreach sales offer numerous advantages for local businesses:

Targeted Approach: Outreach allows us to reach potential clients within their immediate geographical area, making it easier to build strong local customer bases.

Proactive Growth: Businesses can jumpstart growth by actively seeking new clients, rather than relying solely on organic customer acquisition.

Cost-Effective: Outreach sales can be more cost-effective than traditional advertising methods, often requiring fewer financial resources.

Relationship Building: Outreach enables businesses to establish and nurture meaningful client relationships from the start, fostering loyalty and long-term success.

Overcoming Challenges in Outreach Sales

While outreach sales offer significant benefits, they also come with challenges. These include potential rejection, initial reluctance from potential clients and resource constraints such as limited time and manpower. Balancing outreach activities with day-to-day operations can also be a hurdle.

To address these challenges, my team focuses on daily activities rather than outcomes. We measure everything and know how many people we need to speak to daily to convert them into clients. This approach involves focusing on activities, measuring data and tweaking our strategies quarterly.

With effective strategies and proper training, local businesses can overcome these challenges and reap the rewards of outreach sales. My journey has shown that proactive outreach and continuous improvement can drive significant growth and success. Sharing my story and these strategies on social media has resonated with many, especially those who understand the challenges of upskilling staff without proper support.

Growing an Engaged Audience: My Digital Marketing Journey

In the early days of my digital marketing journey, I focused on sharing valuable posts and conducting regular live sessions on Facebook. As of 2024, Facebook remains the largest social media platform, boasting over 3.05 billion monthly active users and 2.085 billion daily active users. Its diverse demographics, spanning all age groups with a balanced gender distribution (57% male, 43% female), make it a critical platform for marketing and audience engagement. By growing an audience on Facebook and providing clear avenues for them to join your email list, you can capture and nurture leads at various stages of the buying journey.

By sharing valuable and educational content, including my experiences with mental health and business, I built a following of engaged audiences, who often shared their own issues. By sharing relatable content, I established trust, converting many of these followers into long-term clients.

Maximising Audience Engagement

Growing your audience and email list ensures you can effectively reach all three types of 'strawberries':

- **Red Strawberries (Ready to Buy):** Target these leads with persuasive offers.
- **Part-Green, Part-Red Strawberries (Warm Leads):** Not ready to buy, but will become ready if we nurture them on our email list and social media content.
- **Green Strawberries (Cold Leads):** Engage them with relevant messaging.

Furthermore, your email list becomes a powerful tool for segmentation and personalisation. You can tailor your marketing messages based on where each contact falls on the 'strawberry spectrum', increasing the likelihood of resonating with their specific needs and preferences. A well-cultivated email list and audience enable you to harness the full potential of your marketing efforts, ensuring no opportunity goes to waste and helping your business thrive in a competitive market.

Diverse Marketing Strategies for Growth

Building an audience through diverse marketing strategies is essential for growth and success:

- **Direct Mail Campaigns:** Craft a compelling message, design an eye-catching mailer with a clear call to action, personalise it and track performance for continuous improvement.
- **Cold Calling:** Conduct thorough research to identify leads, prioritise them and use a tailored script to address their needs.
- **Networking at Events:** Research the event, bring business cards, practice your pitch, engage in genuine conversations and follow up promptly.
- **Print Advertising:** Design compelling ads, choose the right publications and monitor performance to optimise ROI (Return on Investment).
- **Referral Programmes:** Incentivise existing customers to refer new clients by clearly communicating benefits, making it easy to refer others and rewarding promptly.
- **Social Media Presence:** Create a content strategy, choose the right platforms, engage with the audience and use analytics to refine your approach.
- **Local Radio Advertising:** Craft a well-crafted message, choose the right stations and monitor performance.
- **Collaborating with Other Businesses:** Identify complementary partners and propose mutual collaboration ideas.

Measuring Success and Making Incremental Improvements

We experiment with various marketing strategies and continuously adjust our approach based on measured results. For instance, we discovered that cold outreach on social media was ineffective, whereas visiting local salons gave us better results. Attending live events significantly enhanced relationship-building, leading us to focus more on networking events. We constantly analyse what works and what does not, allowing us to make informed decisions and improvements.

Key Metrics for Evaluation

- Conversion Rates
- ROI (Return on Investment)
- Customer Acquisition Cost

Analytical Approaches

We utilise a variety of tools and methodologies to analyse marketing and sales data, ensuring comprehensive insights into our strategies. Ongoing analysis enables us to make incremental improvements in our strategy, ensuring we adapt and refine our approach for optimal results.

The Sales Process

Successful selling starts with direct sales and the art of connecting with customers. The typical sales process involves several key stages:

1. Identifying potential leads through research and networking.
2. Qualifying leads based on budget, need, authority and timeline.
3. Initiating contact through calls, emails or meetings.
4. Assessing needs by engaging in detailed conversations.
5. Presenting your courses as solutions.
6. Handling objections with clear explanations.
7. Closing the sale by finalising terms and securing commitment.
8. Negotiating terms when necessary.
9. Completing paperwork and documentation.
10. Providing follow-up and post-sale support to ensure customer satisfaction.

Conclusion

Understanding your target audience is crucial for tailoring your products, services and marketing efforts to meet their specific needs and preferences. A clear ideal-client profile offers valuable insights into their pain points, desires and behaviours, enabling you to design solutions that directly address their problems and create resonant marketing campaigns. This leads to higher engagement, conversion rates, customer satisfaction and loyalty.

On my journey, I have learned that knowing your ideal client profoundly influences your messaging and branding. It makes your brand more relatable and appealing, enhances brand recognition and trust and increases the likelihood of customers choosing your business over competitors. At TNB Skills, we create different personas for each of our products and dedicate time to researching our perfect client. This ensures that when we speak to potential clients, they can relate to how we can help them.

My story illustrates that with a clear understanding of your target audience and a proactive approach, significant growth and success are achievable.

Chapter 10

Attitude and Mindset

Why talk about attitude and mindset in a book all about funding, you may ask? Here is the reason: after thirty years of business experience, I truly believe that without the right attitude and mindset, you will not survive in business. Statistics published by Hostinger in 2024 claim that only 34% of small businesses survive at least ten years, while 21.9% fail in the first year. Among the failures, 82% experienced cash flow problems, 42% found a lack of demand for their product or service, 29% ran out of cash, 23% did not have the right team and 19% could not beat competitors.

I have faced all these challenges, but I found ways to overcome them, and the only explanation behind this was my attitude and mindset.

Understanding 'mindset' and 'money mindset' is crucial for business owners because these concepts significantly influence decision-making and business strategies. Here is a deeper dive into both terms and how they impact business decisions:

What Is Mindset?

This is a term people throw around, but to me, it refers to the established set of attitudes held by someone. It is the mental framework that shapes our perception of the world around us and determines our reactions to challenges and opportunities. The concept of mindset was popularised by psychologist Carol Dweck, who identified two primary types: fixed and growth.

Fixed Mindset: Individuals believe their abilities, intelligence and talents are fixed traits. They think that success depends on innate talent rather than effort, which might discourage them from taking on new challenges or learning from mistakes.

Growth Mindset: People believe that their abilities and intelligence can be developed through dedication, effort and persistence. This perspective encourages a love of learning and resilience and a drive for self-improvement.

In business, a growth mindset encourages business owners, any business owner, to embrace challenges, persist through obstacles, learn from criticism and find lessons and inspiration in the success of others. This leads to more innovative and flexible business practices.

Money Mindset

A money mindset is a specific subset that refers to one's beliefs and attitudes about money. It affects how individuals earn, save, spend and invest money. Your money mindset can have a profound impact on the financial decisions you make in your business.

Scarcity Mindset: Belief that money is limited. People with a scarcity mindset may hold back on investing in their business due to fear of losing money. They might avoid necessary risks, potentially stunting business growth.

Abundance Mindset: Belief that there is plenty of money to be earned and that more financial opportunities will arise from current investments. This mindset encourages business risk-taking, investment in growth opportunities and a proactive approach to financial challenges.

If I am honest, I have always been fascinated by how the mind works. The dream of owning a successful business and working for myself sparked my journey into self-development, starting in my early twenties. Back then, I dabbled in various side hustles, from network marketing to hosting jewellery and clothing parties, but I struggled to find my true calling. My first real exposure to personal development came in 1994, when a friend, newly affiliated with Amway, invited me, with my husband, to a seminar. Initially sceptical, I was soon captivated by the electric atmosphere and the powerful stories shared on stage. This experience profoundly changed my perspective and ignited my interest in the power of mindset.

Over the years, I immersed myself in personal development, consuming countless tapes and books. While we managed to build a small team in network marketing, I realised it was not the right fit for me. However, this path helped me discover my resilience, which has been invaluable in the training business I run today. From the outset, I was determined to build a million-pound business, often to the amusement of friends who heard me listening to self-help books and podcasts as I transitioned from tapes in the nineties to digital formats in the 2000s.

Despite my dedication, there were periods when I neglected my personal development, and my business suffered. The importance of investing in yourself—through mentors, masterminds and ongoing learning—cannot be overstated. A dear friend and mentor, Pete Cohen, once told me, "You have to become your future self." His words resonated deeply, reinforcing that personal growth is essential, starting with your mindset.

My commitment to personal development was reignited in 2011 after losing a close friend to a brain tumour at just forty-eight. This tragedy was a wake-up call about the futility of my relentless work schedule, which lacked fulfilment.

Fast forward to 2020, and my confidence was at an all-time low. I struggled with isolation and longed for human interaction. Around this time, I discovered an audio app called Clubhouse. This app not only provided networking opportunities but allowed me to connect with entrepreneurs who shared business knowledge.

Through Clubhouse, I met Danny Wicks, a coach who became a long-term mentor. Danny helped me realise the depth of my business acumen, pointing out that my only barriers were confidence and mindset. His guidance was pivotal, empowering me to focus on personal development and overcome these challenges.

Understanding the role of mindset, especially regarding money, is crucial for any business owner. A growth and abundance mindset can enhance your willingness to take calculated risks, crucial for business innovation and growth. Those with a positive money mindset are more likely to invest in marketing, technology or employee development, viewing these costs as investments in the future.

Your mindset affects everything from cash flow and debt management to profit reinvestment or cost-saving measures. Viewing setbacks as learning opportunities, a growth mindset encourages resilience and adaptation, fostering an environment ripe for innovation and scaling. On the other hand, a fixed mindset might limit a business to its comfort zone.

Cultivating a healthy, positive mindset is not just beneficial; it is essential for dynamic, resilient business practices and long-term success.

Personal Development: The Catalyst for Growth

Since the onset of COVID-19, I have dedicated over £250,000 to my personal development. Despite having been in business for over thirty years, I maintain a steadfast belief in the value of lifelong learning. The return on this investment has been extraordinarily rewarding, both personally and professionally. Currently reflecting from a sunbed in Rhodes, where I am inspired to write this chapter, I can affirm that this commitment has paid off significantly. My business now consistently generates between £84,000 to £100,000 in revenue most months, serving as a testament to the notion that investing in oneself is the most profitable investment one can make. The growth and success I have witnessed affirm that focusing on personal development has been the best decision for the longevity and prosperity of my business.

In my quest to enhance my mindset, I have adopted several daily practices that have fundamentally transformed my approach to life and business. Waking up at 5:30 a.m. each day provides the tranquillity and space I need to start my day intentionally. This time is dedicated to meditation and physical activity, which might include a guided podcast session, a walk in the park or a swim. These moments are precious for reflecting upon what truly matters: my family, my friends and even simple comforts like running water.

Recognising these blessings grounds me and bolsters my resilience during challenging business periods. I also carve out time daily for learning, particularly through audiobooks focused on self-development and mindset enhancement. This practice aligns with one of my core values: a Passion for Learning. Each day poses the question, "How can I be better than yesterday?" Embracing this philosophy has not only strengthened my mental resilience but catapulted my business from earning £40,000 a month to £100,000 within just two years.

My journey with money mindset was influenced when I discovered the book *You Are a Badass at Making Money* by Jen Sincero. At the time, I was grappling with a daunting £75,000 in debt and had hit a critical low in business cash flow. Reading Jen's insights prompted a significant shift in how I viewed money, a mindset I continue to refine to this day. Additionally, the teachings of Denise Duffield-Thomas, whose Money Bootcamp I regularly revisit, have been invaluable. I often turn back to her lessons during financial stagnation or when anxiety about money surfaces.

These experiences underscored that desiring more money is not just acceptable; it is essential for achieving broader goals like spending quality time with family and friends and making impactful changes in the world, resonating with Maslow's theory of achieving a purposeful life.

Both Jen Sincero and Denise Duffield-Thomas teach the critical importance of confronting and transforming limiting beliefs about money. For example, the notion that 'money is the root of all evil' can severely restrict someone's financial growth. They help reframe these beliefs to encourage a more positive and powerful money perspective.

They advocate the use of daily affirmations and visualisations to synchronise with the idea of wealth mentally and emotionally. I adopted their techniques, such as visualising my ideal day: envisioning myself in a bungalow in the countryside, relaxing in a garden house, feeling grateful for what we have achieved. This vision stays on my dream board, and excitingly, my husband and I are now viewing a potential bungalow to purchase as I write this book. While visualisation alone does not guarantee results, it certainly shifts your outlook and drives your actions.

Another key practice is to regularly repeat positive money affirmations, which help alter subconscious beliefs and behaviours related to finances. I have reminders on my phone that pop up daily, reinforcing the positive aspects of financial abundance. My biggest hurdle was my spending behaviour. I used to quickly spend any money I made, maxing out credit cards, not saving and consistently spending beyond my earnings.

Reflecting upon this in my journal, I've come to realise that many of my financial behaviours were childhood lessons. My grandparents often reminded me that "money doesn't grow on trees" and emphasised the need to "work hard for money." These early teachings instilled a robust work ethic, but they left me with limiting beliefs about wealth: that I was not truly deserving of financial success unless I worked hard for it. Even now, these old beliefs occasionally resurface, challenging my financial confidence.

Currently, I find myself navigating through one of these challenging periods. This morning, after reflecting upon the content of this book, I turned to the strategies that Denise and Jen have instilled in me. I revisited one of their challenges, which involves setting a goal and breaking down the steps to achieve it within ten days. This approach has reignited my determination to succeed in my latest endeavour.

I am about to launch a comprehensive, six-month, one-to-one mentoring package, priced at £9000 plus VAT. This package not only includes all the courses I have developed but offers six months of personalised mentoring, a year's access to instructional videos and membership to my monthly alumni group. I have set a goal to sell two of these packages in the next ten days and secure full payments upfront.

These moments of doubt are not setbacks but reminders of the ongoing journey in personal and financial development. Each time these limiting beliefs appear, I am equipped with the tools and experiences from money mindset books that guide me back to a path of empowerment and financial affirmation.

These books helped me establish clear and achievable financial goals. Setting these targets isn't just fanciful thinking; it is a strategic approach that drives more focused and effective actions towards financial prosperity.

I believe in business, there are three main stages of business mindset growth. Each revenue level presents its own set of challenges and opportunities, requiring specific mindsets for success. Here is an overview of the mindset needed at each stage:

Stage 1: £0 to £500K - The Entrepreneurial Mindset

At this foundational stage, the key is to cultivate an **entrepreneurial mindset**, which includes:

- **Resilience:** Starting a business can be fraught with setbacks. An entrepreneurial mindset embraces failure as a learning opportunity and perseveres through challenges.
- **Resourcefulness:** With limited resources, being able to make the most of what you have is crucial. This means finding cost-effective solutions and being creative with problem-solving.
- **Adaptability:** The ability to pivot and adapt to market feedback is critical. This means being open to changing your business model or product based on what your early customers are telling you.

Stage 2: £500K to £1 Million – The growth Mindset

Transitioning from survival to growth, entrepreneurs need to develop a **growth mindset**, which focuses on:

- **Strategic Thinking:** Planning not just for immediate needs but for future growth. This includes understanding market trends, potential scale opportunities and the strategic positioning of the business.
- **Delegation:** At this stage, it is essential to start trusting others to take over certain aspects of the business. This involves hiring the right people and empowering them to manage new and existing tasks effectively.
- **Efficiency:** Finding ways to do more with less, whether through technology, optimising operations or streamlining processes. Efficiency is crucial as it supports sustainable growth.

Stage 3: £1 Million & above – The Leadership Mindset

As the business matures further, a **leadership mindset** becomes essential, encompassing:

- **Visionary Thinking:** Being able to set a clear vision and direction for the company's future. This involves anticipating market shifts and setting long-term goals that will position the company as a market leader.

- **Influence and Communication:** Effectively communicating the vision and strategy to stakeholders, including employees, investors and partners, to align efforts and foster commitment.
- **Decision-making:** With the business now more complex, leaders need to make informed, strategic decisions that will impact on the company's trajectory significantly. This requires a deep understanding of the business, its environment and its financial health.

Developing these mindsets is not about personal growth; it is about adapting your approach to meet the evolving needs of your business as it scales. It is a dynamic process that requires ongoing learning, self-awareness, and adjustment.

In navigating the various stages of my business journey, I have incorporated many tools and techniques that have been instrumental to my development. One major influence has been Neuro-Linguistic Programming (NLP), a psychological approach that involves analysing strategies used by successful individuals to achieve personal goals. NLP has helped me reframe my perspectives and manage stress effectively. Another cornerstone of my personal development has been tapping Emotional Freedom Techniques (EFT), a holistic method that combines elements of acupuncture and psychology to alleviate emotional distress and enhance wellness.

However, the journey is not about learning; it is about action. The initial stages of building a business are critical for developing resilience and the tenacity to persevere through challenges. I recall a transformative moment with my mentor Danny, who encouraged me to share my story on social media. Despite my fears of public perception, rooted in childhood experiences of seeking validation, working through these feelings with Danny proved to be a breakthrough. His mentorship over the years has been transformative.

Currently, I work with another mindset coach, Renee Houtsta, included in my mastermind package. Renee emphasises the importance of immediately applying what I learn, not just to my business, but to balancing personal and professional life, a challenge I have struggled with. An insightful discussion with her helped address concerns in my marriage, particularly as my husband felt overshadowed by my business success. Utilising concepts from the book *Love Languages*, Renee helped me understand that recognising and responding to the fundamental emotional needs and love languages of both my spouse and team members can strengthen relationships significantly. By implementing these practices like personalised vouchers for my team, I have not only shown appreciation but promoted a supportive and loyal environment.

Reflecting upon the person you need to become to successfully run your training business is crucial. Ask yourself, “Who is my Future Self?”

For me, the strategy has been to surround myself with business owners whose success I aspire to emulate. There is immense value in being the smallest fish in the pond. By positioning yourself among successful entrepreneurs, you learn extensively through observation, inquiry and engagement. Seek out these individuals, stick with them, ask questions and listen intently. The insights you gain can be transformative.

With that in mind, here are some questions I encourage you to ponder and reflect upon:

What core values must your future self embody to lead a successful business at this scale, and how will these values influence your decision-making processes?

What specific skills and knowledge does your future self need to acquire to manage and scale a business effectively, and what steps are you now taking to develop these?

How does your future self handle setbacks and failures, and what strategies do you have in place to maintain resilience and drive in the face of adversity?

In what ways does your future self prioritise and manage relationships, both professionally and personally, to support a thriving business and a balanced life?

How does your future self stay aligned with the evolving goals of the business while ensuring personal growth and fulfilment?

In this chapter, we have explored the pivotal role of mindset in navigating the complexities of business growth. As my mentor wisely pointed out, the challenges and problems of running a business do not diminish as it grows; they simply evolve and increase in scale. This insight has been crucial in shaping my understanding that continuous personal development, particularly in cultivating a resilient and proactive mindset, is essential. He emphasised that whenever you find yourself stuck, the most effective strategy is to return to mindset work. This approach not only prepares you to tackle the immediate hurdles but lays a robust foundation for future challenges. Thus, the essence of this chapter is to underscore that the right attitude and a proactive mindset are integral not just to personal growth but to weaving these lessons into every facet of life, thereby enriching both personal and professional realms.

I just want to finish with this: “Next year, we will make a million!” It is something I have always said to myself. Jayne, a long-time member of my team, reminded me of this just a few weeks ago, and it brought things into perspective.

Starting my training academy was more than a business venture; it was a mission driven by a clear vision.

I poured endless hours and every pound back into the business. Yes, there were moments of stress, burnout and massive losses that made even my closest friends question if it was all worth it.

Adapting was part of the journey, whether it was government changes throwing us curveballs or sales techniques falling flat. But every setback taught us something vital and pushed us to innovate and persevere.

This year, not only did we hit that million mark, but our profits soared beyond expectations.

Here is what I have learned from my own journey: consistency is key, and believing in your vision is crucial. Investing in yourself, particularly in how you think about money, can transform your life. Most importantly, find a mentor who has successfully navigated the path you are on. The insights and guidance of someone who has been there before are invaluable. I can assure you that the initial investment in a good mentor will repay itself many times over, provided you are willing to put in the necessary work.

Stay focused on your goals and never give up, no matter how challenging the journey might seem. Remember to savour the process and embrace each step of the way. This approach has not only fuelled my success but enriched my life immeasurably. I encourage you to do the same and watch how it can change your world.

Chapter 11

Policies and Procedures

There are many policies and procedures you need before you can bid for your first contract. This chapter provides an overview of the most common ones (although each contract may have specific requirements).

Creating these policies and procedures isn't just about ticking boxes; it is about ensuring your approach genuinely puts learners first. The policies and processes you implement should be both strategically and operationally effective. They need to work together to create a seamless, quality framework that meets good practice standards and can stand up to scrutiny during visits or audits. This focus on quality and compliance has been crucial in my experience and success.

Here is a list of the most common policies and procedures you must have:

- Safeguarding and child protection
- Prevent and British values
- Safer recruitment
- Equality, diversity and inclusion/equal opportunities
- Additional learning needs/additional learning support, including special consideration and reasonable adjustments
- Health and safety (plus risk assessments)
- Overarching quality document for internal quality assurance
- Staff professional development (CPD)
- Complaints procedure, including details of how to contact the ESFA
- Data protection/GDPR, including privacy notices and document and data retention
- Conflict of interest
- Opposing bribery and corruption
- Public interest and disclosure: whistleblowing
- Opposing fraud
- Professional code of conduct
- Plan for continuity of training
- Learner handbook
- Staff handbook
- Information, advice, guidance and admissions
- Attendance and punctuality

- Learner grievance, disciplinary and appeals
- Bullying and harassment
- Assessment malpractice and maladministration
- Environmental sustainability

Remember to assign someone to be responsible for all policies and procedures, ensuring they are updated at least annually (or more frequently if legislation changes). We learned this the hard way when our Ofsted visit was almost impacted by not informing new managers about these updates. Luckily, a last-minute check revealed our safeguarding policy needed updating and we quickly fixed it. This incident highlighted the importance of having a checklist and following these procedures.

The following are examples of policies you will need in place:

Safeguarding

In my experience, safeguarding and child protection have always been paramount. The statutory guidance, 'Keeping Children Safe in Education' (KCSIE), which is updated annually, underscores this priority. Schools, colleges and training providers in England are mandated to maintain an up-to-date safeguarding and child protection policy, aligning with KCSIE to safeguard and promote the welfare of children. For safeguarding purposes, children and young people are defined as any learners under the age of eighteen, and adults who are considered at risk are also included.

It is crucial to understand that safeguarding should not be a mere tick-box exercise but deeply embedded in your provision, especially when working with anyone eighteen or below. According to the current Ofsted framework, safeguarding is a limiting grade. This means that even if all other aspects of your provision are outstanding, failure to embed safeguarding throughout your organisation can lower your overall grade to 'Unsatisfactory'. An unsatisfactory grade often results in being unable to bid for contracts or work as a subcontractor or partner.

Prevent

The Prevent duty and the promotion of British values are also critical components of our safeguarding efforts. The Prevent duty aims to ensure that all staff, customers and learners feel safe and are protected from threats related to extremism and radicalisation. Education providers must effectively monitor, manage and address threats posed by any individual or group engaged in violent extremism, in alignment with the Prevent duty guidance and Section 26(1) of the Counter-Terrorism and Security Act 2015, updated as of April 1, 2021.

British Values

British values encompass respect for the rule of law, individual liberty, democracy and mutual respect and tolerance for different faiths and beliefs. Promoting these values is part of the government's initiative to foster a cohesive and integrated society and to protect children from extremist ideologies. It is very important that all your staff must hold current, valid safeguarding and Prevent training certificates

To ensure a comprehensive and cohesive approach to safeguarding, prevention and promoting British values, our organisation, TNB Skills, has implemented a structured process. The safeguarding officer is responsible for ensuring all staff members hold current, valid safeguarding and Prevent training certificates. This is achieved through monthly training sessions conducted via online resources to ensure accessibility and convenience. Additionally, weekly team meetings are held to discuss training progress, address any issues and reinforce the principles of British values, safeguarding and Prevent. Tutors are required to demonstrate how these principles are incorporated into their lessons, fostering an educational environment that upholds these values. The safeguarding officer regularly reviews and assesses the effectiveness of the training and its implementation, collecting feedback from staff and students to continuously improve the process.

Safer Recruitment

On my journey, I've learned that safer recruitment is essential for ensuring that staff and volunteers are suitable to work with children and young people. This practice is crucial for creating a safe and positive environment and demonstrates a genuine commitment to protecting children from harm.

A safer recruitment policy statement is a key component of your overall safeguarding policies and procedures. It clearly expresses your organisation's dedication to recruiting staff and volunteers who are fit to work with children. This policy sends a strong message to staff, volunteers and potential applicants that your organisation prioritises the safety and welfare of children.

Your policy statement should reflect your organisation's commitment to:

- Safeguarding and protecting all children and young people through rigorous safer recruitment practices.
- Identifying and rejecting applicants who are unsuitable to work with children and young people.
- Addressing concerns about the suitability of applicants during the recruitment process.
- Responding to concerns about the suitability of employees and volunteers once they have started their role.
- Ensuring all new staff and volunteers undergo an induction that includes child protection.
- Providing a list of supporting procedures that accompany the policy.
- Stating the date the policy takes effect and when it will be reviewed.

Your safer recruitment policy statement should complement other policies within your organisation, such as your equal opportunities policy, and be part of your broader safeguarding policy framework. To ensure this happens and to stay as current as possible, you must also ensure all your team who have contact with learners must hold a current Enhanced Disclosure and Barring Service Check that is updated regularly.

Equality, Diversity and Inclusion (EDI)/Equal Opportunities

Throughout my training provider journey, I have come to understand the importance of equality, diversity and inclusion (EDI) in creating a supportive and inclusive learning environment. The Equality Act 2010 protects nine specific characteristics:

- Age
- Disability
- Gender reassignment
- Marriage and civil partnership
- Pregnancy and maternity
- Race
- Religion or belief
- Sex
- Sexual orientation

As training providers, you have a duty to actively promote equality of opportunity. To fulfil opportunity, staff need to be aware of the limits of their responsibilities and know when and where to access support for themselves and their learners. This applies not only to protected characteristics but to learners' additional learning and social needs and an awareness of stereotyping prejudice and unconscious bias.

Equality in education is not about treating everyone the same; it is about giving everyone an equal opportunity to access the learning experience.

Diversity is about celebrating people's differences, such as backgrounds, knowledge, skills and experiences, and using those differences to enrich the learning experience.

Inclusion is the practice of ensuring that all people feel they belong, are engaged and relate to the group.

Why EDI Is So Important

Equality and diversity are crucial because they create an environment where all learners can thrive. Your team need to be educated about how different protected characteristics can be affected if not approached with sensitivity and awareness. For instance, using inclusive language is essential to avoid offending individuals and creating barriers to learning. Instead of saying, "Good morning, ladies and gentlemen," you might say, "Good morning, everyone," ensuring that no one feels excluded or marginalised, particularly those from the LGBTQ+ community.

To cultivate an inclusive environment that prevents discrimination and ensures every learner feels valued and respected, we require all team members to hold current, valid equality and diversity training certificates.

This initiative enhances the learning experience and promotes a culture of acceptance.

To maintain this standard, our team is required to regularly attend training sessions. These sessions include both online and team-based training, ensuring that everyone is updated with the latest requirements of the law and government policies.

All training records are held in a central file, accessible to stakeholders and funders during their visits. By following this process, we can create a supportive and inclusive environment for all learners.

Additional Learning Needs/Additional Learning Support

Some learners may require modified assessments to meet their individual needs. This process, known as reasonable adjustments and/or special consideration, must be outlined in a policy that details how you will accommodate additional learning needs (ALN) and additional learning support (ALS).

Equity, in simple terms, means distributing resources based on the needs of the recipients rather than giving everyone the same resources. In practice, this could mean providing extra time in exams for learners with dyslexia, scribing for a learner who has a disability or injury that prevents them from writing, or offering assistive technology to enable staff or learners to fully participate and engage with teaching, learning, assessments and everyday activities within their organisation.

Awarding organisations provide guidance on appropriate, reasonable adjustments that approved centres can make. They support centres in implementing these adjustments to ensure that learners can demonstrate their attainment and compensate for any disadvantage imposed by their disability, without giving them an unfair advantage.

It is essential for awarding organisations to be informed of any reasonable adjustments made. This includes completing and submitting all relevant documentation to ensure transparency and compliance.

By embracing these practices, we ensure that every learner has the support they need to succeed, reflecting our commitment to an inclusive and equitable learning environment.

Health and Safety (Including Risk Assessments)

I have learned that managing health and safety is not just a legal requirement but a fundamental aspect of creating a safe learning environment. The law mandates that every business must have a policy for managing health and safety. This policy outlines your general approach to health and safety, detailing how you as an employer will manage it within your business. It should clearly state who does what, when and how. If you employ more than five people, this policy must be documented in writing.

As a training provider, regardless of the number of employees, your health and safety policy and procedures must be in writing and are essential for bidding on contracts. You must demonstrate how you will keep learners safe, including wider documentation such as risk assessments, Control of Substances Hazardous to Health (COSHH), Reporting of Incidents, Diseases and Dangerous Occurrences Regulations (RIDDOR) and portable appliance testing (PAT), which is the term used to describe the examination of electrical appliances and equipment to ensure they are safe to use.

Given that the goal of most of our training provisions is to ensure that learners can progress into employment, it is crucial to address the health and safety aspects of external work environments. Since you will often be working with outside employers, you must ensure that any learners participating in work experience are also properly overseen. This includes conducting thorough risk assessments and ensuring all relevant health and safety measures are in place at the employer's premises.

One of the things we do is ensure all staff who carry out health and safety assessments on premises hold an Institution of Occupational Safety and Health Certificate. You must also have an adequate number of trained first aiders, depending on the size of your organisation. By embedding these practices, we not only comply with legal requirements but foster a safe and supportive environment that helps learners to transition smoothly into the workforce.

Staff Professional Development (CPD)

One of my core values is a Passion for Learning, which has been pivotal in motivating my team and ensuring they reach their full potential. Anyone joining my business who does not share this passion is unlikely to stay long, as it is vital for our success. Moreover, it is a requirement for Ofsted, awarding bodies and outside stakeholders.

Learning and development are essential elements of professional life. Development targets not only enhance employees' sector knowledge, skills and performance but address the needs of individual employees, the business, our customers and the communities we serve.

Your policy should outline how you will provide staff with appropriate training to develop the sector knowledge, skills and performance necessary for them to perform their duties effectively. Wherever possible, you should also demonstrate how you will ensure opportunities for career development.

Include specific requirements for induction and mandatory training, such as safeguarding, Prevent, GDPR and E&D, and specify how often these must be refreshed.

Awarding organisations also stipulate minimum annual requirements for CPD for all teaching, assessing and quality assurance staff. Your policy must detail these requirements. For example, VTCT requires all assessing and IQA (internal quality assurer) staff to undertake a minimum of thirty to fifty hours of sector-specific vocational training every year, depending on the qualifications they are assessing or ensuring the quality of. To ensure compliance, we recommend setting sector vocational CPD to a minimum requirement of fifty hours per year.

By embedding a strong culture of continuous professional development, we not only comply with external requirements but cultivate an environment where our team thrives, benefiting our learners and stakeholders.

Complaints Procedure, Including ESFA Contact Details

As a business committed to the core value of 'Above and Beyond' as standard, receiving complaints can be disheartening. However, as you grow, it is inevitable that some clients may feel their expectations were not met. The key is not to dwell on these moments but to learn from them. Having a clear complaints procedure will help your organisation by turning challenges into learning opportunities.

You must have a written complaints procedure published on your website. This procedure should detail the process for making a formal complaint, including how to appeal a complaints decision and how to contact the ESFA if they wish to escalate the complaint. If you are a subcontractor, the procedure must also include details on how to complain to your lead/main provider.

Data Protection/General Data Protection Regulation GDPR, Including Privacy Notices and Document and Data Retention

As a training provider, it is essential to ensure that information is accurate, secure and in line with data protection regulations to maintain a clear audit trail. Understanding the need for strict security of learner data and assessment results is crucial. You are responsible for the security and confidentiality of learner data, enrolment records and all assessment materials, including examination question papers, examination scripts, marking records and portfolios of evidence before, during and after assessments.

Any security breaches must be reported immediately to the Information Commissioners Office (ICO), if appropriate, and to the awarding organisation. Compliance with GDPR is mandatory.

You must have documented processes for record-keeping and maintain copies of important information. All documentation related to the delivery and assessment of qualifications must be securely stored and readily accessible for inspection by regulatory authorities and awarding organisations. All staff must also hold data protection and GDPR training certificates that are updated accordingly as and when new regulations are introduced and saved in a central file where stakeholders and funders can access them if needed.

By implementing these practices, you ensure that your organisation not only meets regulatory requirements but fosters a culture of transparency, accountability and continuous improvement.

Conflict of Interest

This policy sets out responsibilities for meeting the requirements of awarding organisations for recognising where a conflict of interest may arise and setting out how you mitigate the risks in these instances. There may be situations when a perceived or potential conflict of interest may arise, and we therefore have a duty to identify, manage and mitigate potential conflicts of interest.

For the purpose of your policy, a conflict of interest is defined as a situation in which an individual or organisation has, or may be perceived to have, competing interests or loyalties which could lead to a potentially subjective, biased or corrupt decision being made by that individual or organisation.

In some circumstances, conflicts of interest may also constitute a form of corruption, so you will also need a policy against bribery and corruption.

In practice, a conflict of interest is where a learner may receive preferential treatment, such as where:

- Staff members are completing qualifications in-house for CPD or training purposes.
- A learner is known to the assessor and/or IQA.
- The assessor and IQA are related in some way.

Anti-bribery and anti-corruption policies

This policy must set out your commitment to conducting all your business in an honest and ethical manner, demonstrating that you will not tolerate any acts of bribery or corruption and that you are committed to acting professionally and ethically in all business dealings and relationships. It shows commitment to implementing and enforcing effective systems to counter bribery and ensures that employees are aware of their duties towards the company: to report and help to prevent any acts of bribery or corruption across the organisation.

Public Interest and Disclosure: Whistleblowing

This policy should demonstrate how you safeguard and act in the interest of the public and your staff. It must explain how any fraud, misconduct or wrongdoing by employees or other agents should be reported and properly addressed.

It should encourage bringing to the attention of the company any practice or action of the company, its employees or other agents that someone reasonably believes is against the public interest, in that the practice or action is a criminal offence, a failure to comply with any legal obligation, a miscarriage of justice, a danger to the health and safety of any individual or an attempt to conceal information on any of the above.

You must ensure that any individual raising legitimate concerns will not be subject to any detriment, either during or after employment, and endeavour to ensure that the individual is protected from any intimidation or harassment by any other parties.

Opposing Fraud

As a publicly funded training provider, you are responsible for the detection and prevention of fraud, misappropriations and other irregularities. Fraud is defined as the intentional, false representation or concealment of a material fact for the purpose of inducing another to act upon it to his or her injury.

Your anti-fraud policy should facilitate the development of controls that will aid in the detection and prevention of fraud, promoting consistent organisational behaviour by providing guidelines and assigning responsibility for the development of controls and conduct of investigations.

Professional Code of Conduct

Your code of conduct or professional ethics policy should clearly outline the expectations for employee behaviour and interactions with learners, considering the age, gender and maturity of everyone. It is crucial to ensure that all aspects of demeanour, language and attitudes are clear and unambiguous to prevent misunderstandings, especially when interacting with adolescent boys and girls. Avoiding ambiguous or ambivalent comments and conduct is particularly important.

The policy should address various areas, including:

- Physical contact
- Corporal punishment
- Private meetings
- First aid
- Comments and discussions with learners
- Infatuations and crushes
- Off-site activities
- Teaching materials
- Personal communications
- Reporting incidents

Plan for Continuity of Training

All publicly funded training contracts require a flexible and comprehensive plan detailing how to respond to emergencies or disruptive incidents, ensuring the continuity of training. This plan should aim to:

- Minimise the impact of an emergency, major incident or pandemic.
- Communicate the emergency incident quickly and clearly to supporting agencies and partners, enabling rapid activation of support arrangements.
- Maintain high standards of welfare and duty of care for learners, staff and carers.

- Ensure that decision-making and actions during the emergency are properly recorded.
- Minimise educational and administrative disruption.
- Facilitate the return to normal working arrangements as soon as possible.
- Plan for the continuity of training for learners in the event that the organisation can no longer trade due to administration or liquidation, or if it is unable to meet training contract obligations directly or through subcontracts.

This really helped us in 2020 when Covid pandemic hit and having a step-by-step process will also give you peace of mind, even if you never need to use it

Learner Handbook

Your learner handbook will be required for contracts and for awarding body approvals. It should contain, as a minimum, course information; entry/enrolment requirements; possible progression routes; things learners need to bring to lessons; ground rules and expectations of learners; details of the centre staff; appeals procedures; disciplinary procedures, including gross misconduct and reasons for removal from a course; complaints procedure; equal opportunities policy; arrangements for additional learning needs and additional learning support; availability of bursary financial support; safeguarding procedures; and arrangements and details of the designated safeguarding officers.

Staff Handbook

Your staff/employee handbook should contain all of your employment policies, including, but not limited to, safeguards and standards; data protection and GDPR; email and internet use; social media use; standards of behaviour and dress code; capability, disciplinary and grievance; health and safety, including use of alcohol and drugs; fitness to work; statutory pay and leave entitlements; equality, diversity and inclusion; anti-bribery policies; whistleblowing; dealing with a pandemic; bullying and harassment; and termination of employment.

Information, Advice and Guidance and Admissions

You must have a policy that demonstrates how you recognise the learner's need to be on the right course, at the right time and with appropriate support in order to achieve their chosen qualifications. Training providers have moral and ethical obligations to ensure all learners are recruited with integrity and to provide appropriate information, advice and guidance free of charge to all learners within a reasonable timeframe.

Your admissions policy should be transparent about entry requirements and minimum standards for progression routes, such as expected attendance and punctuality percentages.

Attendance and Punctuality

You must be able to demonstrate that you set and expect high standards with regards to attendance and punctuality for all learners, and that you identify and address any problems that impede punctuality and regular attendance.

If there are problems that affect a learner's attendance or punctuality, you must investigate, identify and strive, in partnership with parents/carers, support workers and learners, to resolve these problems as quickly and efficiently as possible. A clearly focused approach must be adopted, detailed in a pastoral support plan, aimed at returning the learner to full attendance. A similar approach must be adopted with learners whose punctuality is considered to be an issue.

Your policy should set clear targets, absence reporting procedures and guidelines for staff, to help them deal with poor attendance and punctuality and state where they can access appropriate support.

Learner grievance, disciplinary action and appeals

You must have procedures in place for learners, stating how they can raise a grievance, including how to appeal any decision made and a procedure for when and how disciplinary action may be taken against a learner. This should include examples of gross misconduct, which may result in instant removal from a training course, such as being under the influence of drugs or alcohol at the training centre or on employer premises.

You must also have a documented learner appeals procedure, stating how a learner can appeal an assessment decision. This must include the stages of appeal, from assessor through to IQA, and finally to the awarding organisation/external quality assurer.

Opposing Bullying and Harassment

Everyone has the right to work and learn in a secure and caring environment. You must commit to implementing appropriate action to tackle the mistreatment of others by preventing and acting upon any form of bullying towards learners, staff and visitors. Zero tolerance of bullying must be actively promoted via all training provider policies. Your anti-bullying and anti-harassment policy should be central to a whole range of other policies and should therefore be applied in conjunction with those policies. Such policies include equality and diversity, behaviour guidelines, safeguarding and child protection, health & safety, whistle blowing and staff code of professional conduct.

Assessment Malpractice and Maladministration

The objectives of this policy are to protect the quality and credibility of the qualifications system and demonstrate how you mitigate and deal with instances of malpractice and maladministration.

Malpractice is the term used for any action, activity, neglect, default or other practice which deliberately contravenes regulations and compromises the integrity of the internal or external assessment process, the validity of results and/or certificates, or the reputation and credibility of awarding bodies or the wider qualification community.

Maladministration is any activity, neglect, default or other practice that results in non-compliance with awarding body requirements or any other applicable requirements and includes the occurrence of persistent mistakes or poor administration within a centre. Recurrent maladministration constitutes malpractice and will be treated as such by awarding bodies.

Insurance Policies

To deliver publicly funded government training, you must hold insurance with the minimum cover values shown below:

- Employers Liability: £10 million
- Public Liability: £10 million
- Professional Indemnity: £5 million

Additionally, it is recommended that you should have insurance cover in place to protect directors, owners and key personnel in the event of an accident or illness. This demonstrates a commitment to providing continuity of training in unforeseen circumstances and can be included in your continuity plan.

As well as all the above policies and procedures, to gain a contract, you must have the following in place and readily available for all to see:

Sustainability

As the UK moves towards a net zero emissions target by 2050, the government and local authorities are placing more emphasis on effective sustainability policies as part of the criteria for successful contract bids. In business, sustainability refers to conducting operations without negatively impacting the environment, community or society as a whole. Sustainability in business addresses two main categories: the effect business has on the environment and the effect business has on society.

In education and training, some suggested policy objectives are:

- Promote responsibility for the environment within the organisation and communicate and implement this policy at all levels within the workforce and learning community.
- Reduce the use of energy, water and other resources.
- Minimise waste through reducing, reusing and recycling methods.
- Comply with all relevant environmental legislation and regulations.
- Ensure that all policies and services are developed in a way that complements this policy.

- Do not prioritise funding needs ahead of sustainability requirements.
- Identify and provide appropriate training, advice and information for staff and learners, encouraging them to develop new ideas and initiatives.
- Provide appropriate resources to meet the commitments of this policy.
- Promote and encourage involvement in local environmental initiatives and schemes.
- Embrace opportunities for digital learning to reduce the need for travel.
- Encourage the use of public transport, cycle-to-work schemes and car-sharing initiatives.
- Develop flexible training solutions to provide opportunities to the whole community, supporting the local society as a whole.

To bid successfully, it is not enough to simply create a policy and an action plan; you need to be able to demonstrate your commitment to reducing your carbon footprint and detail how you plan to achieve this. The most effective way to do this is by signing up to a carbon management platform such as Greenly:

https://greenly.earth/en-gb

The cost of a service like Greenly is in the region of £199 per month for the basic assessment, rising to around £4,000 per year for comprehensive and ongoing measurement and support. For the enhanced fee, they will support you in assessing, managing and sustainably reducing your CO2 emissions. The full package allows you to measure emission data more accurately and work with them to identify a range of actions to reduce your carbon footprint towards net zero. The platform also enables you to measure your suppliers' emissions, helping you make more informed choices about who you work with, including an analysis of your supply chain and the local businesses within it. Additionally, you can offset the emissions you can't reduce by contributing to Greenly-certified projects, provided by accredited and certified partners for both local and international projects.

Systems and Procedures

Having the right processes and systems is the backbone of our operations. Incorporating these from the beginning will save you a significant amount of time in the future. Government funding often entails many audits, and having efficient systems in place will increase your productivity, ensuring you are always ready for government audits & Ofsted inspections. I must warn you, there are many audits, and I wish we had invested in these systems sooner. Not having them reduced my profits and growth, and there was so much room for error, which has cost me a lot. For example, during an ESFA (Education and Skills Funding Agency) audit, my overtime costs skyrocketed because my team had to find data that should have been readily available. This nearly cost us our contract and forced us to stop running a particular course because the tutor assessor could not provide evidence of learning, off-the-job training, and reviews, which are part of the funding rules criteria.

When we started, we had a simple written learner journey, beginning from the engagement of the new learner to their exit.

We shared this with our entire team and are now sharing with our mentee associate satellites and work-based trainers.

Our team regularly refers to it when unsure of the next steps. It needs tweaking yearly as systems change, but it has consistently helped new and old team members alike, and has served as a quick reference when we have not handled something for a while. It is an easy resource to send to your team and associates when they have questions. However, having automated systems that are easy to use and can pull up data has reduced costs and makes it easier to measure what is and is not working. Since we are heavily measured on achievements, retention and satisfaction from learners and businesses we work with, this is where we started.

Investing in automated management systems has made a massive difference for us. Here are some systems we now use, but you should do your own research as there are many options. I highly recommend speaking to your competition to understand the pros and cons of each. There are many systems out there, but I would start with a marketing and sales system. We currently use a white-labelled product built on the Go High Level system and work with a tech wizard. This not only helps us generate leads but helps us measure our marketing and sales numbers, which is crucial: it allows my sales team to respond efficiently. We recently added Wati to our system, which has been a game-changer for responding to our messages and well worth the investment.

Next is a learner management system. There are many on the market, but we use one called PICS. This system is like your customer journey. Jobs that used to take my team hours to do manually now take only five minutes. It also helps reduce costs, making the business more profitable. The upfront investment is well worth the time and will save you in the long run. Another system I can recommend is Aptem, which is a bit more expensive but something we might switch to as the business grows.

We have also recently introduced a project management tool called Motion; an AI (Artificial Intelligence) tool that helps us manage all our projects. We have broken it down into Strategy, Marketing, Sales, Quality, Operations and Finance. It automatically schedules tasks in diaries and assigns tasks to each team member, reducing the need for many meetings and keeping us on track with our goals. As I draft this book, we have only used it with senior management and a few members of the team, but we plan to roll it out to the entire team. I believe this will improve profitability and help prioritise tasks within timelines and improve productivity.

But if you're not quite there yet, using a written journey that all your team can refer to is a starting point: we have one for all aspects of the business and all admin tasks.

It includes customer journey admissions, onboarding, on programme and exit of each funding stream. The list I provided is not exhaustive, but covers the essentials. As a funded training provider, it is crucial to revisit compliance regularly. This is why most training businesses employ a compliance team to oversee adherence and stay updated with any changes. Therefore, when planning your training business, it's important to consider this aspect to ensure your team grows to be as effective as possible.

Human Resources Procedures

Our HR procedures cover everything from recruitment and selection to employee onboarding, performance appraisals, and handling disciplinary or grievance issues. We also make sure to promote equal opportunity and diversity across the board. Every team member gets an employee handbook to refer to, which includes all these procedures. The best part? Our HR department, which we outsource, keeps it up to date, ensuring we're always compliant with the latest laws and regulations—these rules change constantly, so having someone specialised in this area has been a lifesaver. Honestly, I can't recommend this enough!

Financial Procedures

I've already touched on a lot of this in the funding chapter, so I'll keep it brief here. Having someone who truly loves numbers has been a huge relief for me. Julie, our financial director, creates these easy-to-read graphs that I can check weekly to stay on track. But beyond that, having written procedures in place for budgeting and financial planning, expense reporting and reimbursement, payroll processing, invoicing, accounts receivable, accounts payable, and purchasing is a game changer. It makes any transition smooth if someone from the team leaves. The best part? You don't have to write these all by yourself. I get my team to draft them as they go about their daily tasks, and we keep everything neatly filed under each department in our staff training files.

Information Technology Procedures

We outsource all of our IT needs to a specialist, which has been a real lifesaver. One of the big requirements for securing government funding is having strong cybersecurity measures in place. In the UK, cybersecurity is all about protecting sensitive data from breaches and ensuring our systems are secure—especially when it comes to education. We're regularly audited by an outside agency, and we have to share all this information with the Education Skills Funding Agency. Without meeting these strict cybersecurity standards, we wouldn't even be able to get a contract.

Our IT partner handles everything for us, including data backup and recovery, IT support and troubleshooting, network security, and even regular software updates and patch management. They keep us compliant, safe, and running smoothly, which takes a huge weight off our shoulders.

Customer Service Procedures

I've already covered much of this in our earlier policies & procedures, including the Learner journey, customer handbook, and grievance procedures. But on top of that, we have a customer complaints sheet that the senior management team reviews regularly. It's amazing what you can learn from these things and how they can help you put better systems in place. Having a clear customer complaints procedure that everyone can see is such a positive tool. We also make a point of doing regular surveys and asking students to complete a case study form at the end of their courses. This not only helps us gather testimonials but has also done wonders for our Google reviews.

We've also got procedures in place for product returns and refunds, and we always take customer feedback seriously, whether it's through surveys or direct comments. All of this really helps us keep improving and ensuring our customers are happy.

Marketing and Sales Procedures

This procedure covers lead generation and management, the sales process and follow-up, and marketing campaigns and promotions, which I've detailed in the marketing and sales chapter of the book. When I first started, all of this was just in my head, but writing it down and creating clear training plans for my team made a world of difference. Having courses for them to follow and detailed info on all our products and services has allowed me to grow my marketing and sales team to five revenue-producing members. It's saved me so much time and made our processes way more efficient.

Training and Development Procedures

Being a training provider has definitely been an advantage for us. Having the apprenticeship standards in place has provided us with clear processes and procedures. As I've mentioned and documented in the Dream Team chapter, we've put in place solid employee training programs and continuous professional development.

One tool I haven't touched on yet is our skill assessments and training needs analysis tool. The senior management team regularly scores this, and everyone is given clear KPIs and written job descriptions. Managers incorporate this into their 1-2-1 meetings with each team member, ensuring everything is documented with clear development plans.

We even ask our team to score themselves against our company values and explain how they've lived up to them. I believe this approach motivates them, makes them feel part of something bigger, and really builds trust.

Environmental Procedures

As I've already mentioned in the policies section, signing up with Greenly has been a game-changer for maintaining our sustainability efforts. It provides us with clear procedures for waste management and recycling, energy conservation, and environmental impact assessments. I can't recommend it enough—it saves us so much time and resources. Yes, there's a cost involved, but it's totally worth it considering how much time and effort we'd spend if we didn't have this support. Plus, it helps us stay on top of all our sustainability goals.

Looking back on my journey, I've realized that having strong policies and procedures isn't just about ticking boxes—it's about laying the groundwork for real success. Every policy, whether it's about safety or sustainability, is key to creating a learning environment that's safe, inclusive, and runs smoothly. These guidelines don't just help us stay on the right side of the law; they also show our commitment to doing things right and constantly improving. By carefully crafting and putting these frameworks in place, I've been able to build a training organisation that not only meets the required standards but also promotes a culture of acceptance and quality, meeting the diverse needs of all our learners. This thorough approach has been a big part of my success, and I believe it's essential for any organisation that wants to thrive in the education sector.

Chapter 12

Summary of the Book

As we wrap up this book, my aim has been to help you confidently seek funding and develop a clear strategy on how and when to use it. The goal is to build a sustainable training business with recurring revenue streams and multiple funding sources, including contracts from other training providers, the government, and local councils.

By covering the basics of running a funded training business—like mission, vision, and core values—I hope I've shown you why these elements are crucial as you scale. They not only attract the right funders but also guide your business growth. We've discussed managing your financial health to secure larger bids and retain funding, understanding the different funding pots available, and knowing where and how to bid for them. I've explained the differences between accredited and regulated training and how these can increase your chances of winning bids and boosting the value of your business.

We've also touched on the importance of building a dream team, transitioning into the CEO role to steer the business instead of doing all the work yourself, and creating the time and financial freedom to enjoy life. Having a clear marketing and sales strategy is essential to attract funders and clients, and it's crucial to spend the funds you're awarded effectively. As your business grows from five to seven figures and beyond, you'll need to adopt different mindsets and ensure your processes and systems run smoothly, even in your absence.

This will set you up for a scalable business that you can eventually sell at a premium price when you retire.

Remember, there are countless funding opportunities out there—not just in education. By mastering the tendering process and learning how to write winning bids, you'll be well-equipped to tap into various funding pots. For example, we have managed to reclaim £48,000 in R&D funding for our new digital course products this year.

Research and Development funding is financial support provided to encourage innovation by funding activities that involve research into new knowledge or technologies and turning these ideas into practical applications. In the UK, R&D funding can come from various sources, like government grants, tax credits, and subsidies. It's particularly valuable for businesses because it reduces the financial risk associated with innovation and often comes with additional perks like access to research facilities or collaboration opportunities. Without our tendering & knowledge of funding, I truly believe we would not have stumbled on this £48,000, which I believe will be spent more wisely than by any of today's governments.

I hope you now have a clearer understanding of the funded training landscape and how to navigate it. We've covered everything from securing funding to setting up a successful training business. My goal has been to simplify the process and show you that, despite the complexities and red tape, securing funding for your training programmes is not only possible but also incredibly rewarding.

I believe strongly in collaboration and sharing knowledge to help each other grow. That is why I have put my experience and insights into this book—to provide you with a roadmap to success. Whether you're just starting out or looking to expand your existing training business, the strategies and tips shared here are designed to help you achieve your goals and feel part of a supportive community.

If you're ready to dive deeper into funding your training programmes, I invite you to join me in my 'Preparing for funding' packages. These courses will guide you through the process, offering personalised support to ensure you can secure funding and grow your business. You'll learn how to develop compelling training programmes, navigate the red tape, and build a sustainable revenue stream—all with our ongoing support.

To get started, visit my website at:
https://howtofundmycourses.com/book
and sign up for the course.

Together, we can turn your training business dreams into reality, allowing you to focus on delivering high-quality training while we handle the bureaucratic side.

Thanks for joining me on this journey. I am excited to help you succeed and achieve remarkable things in funded training.

About The Author

With over 25 years of business experience, Sarah Abel has developed comprehensive training programs, leveraging government funding to train both new and existing team members in a wide range of skills, including hair, nails, beauty, customer service, teaching mentoring management & digital marketing. These programs were instrumental in building a highly skilled, motivated, and loyal team, which played a crucial role in scaling six of her service-based businesses to six figures, including her own training business, which grew to seven figures.

Sarah's work has earned her the prestigious Matrix Standard, and she has been nominated for and won several business awards. She has secured multiple government contracts to deliver free funded training to thousands, including apprenticeships, government loans, and grants. Sarah is passionate about helping others do the same.

Her entire team has trained using these funding opportunities, and she now leads a group of experts in HR, finance compliance, sales, marketing, and qualified teachers and mentors. Sarah is on a mission to share her proven strategies with other business founders, helping them replicate her success, reclaim their time and money, and build a legacy they can be proud of.

Find more at:

linkedin.com/company/tnbskillstraining/about

instagram.com/tnbhairandbeauty_

facebook.com/tnbskillstraining

Printed in Great Britain
by Amazon

52195798R00128